READING THE BIBLE FOR THE FIRST TIME

Outlook Books

HOW TO READ THE BIBLE
based on the Good News Bible
John Goldingay

BY ALL MEANS
New approaches to group Bible Study
William Metcalf

O MY PEOPLE
God's call to society
John Ferguson

Other titles in preparation

READING THE BIBLE FOR THE FIRST TIME

John Goldingay

Judson Press, ® Valley Forge

READING THE BIBLE FOR THE FIRST TIME

Published by Judson Press, Valley Forge, PA 19481, in 1979.

First published as *How to Read the Bible* by OLIPHANTS, Marshall, Morgan and Scott, a member of the Pentos group, 1 Bath Street, London, EC1V 9LB, 1977.

 Printed in the U.S.A.

CONTENTS

ACKNOWLEDGEMENTS

I am indebted to my colleague Dr Stephen Travis for commenting on the parts of this book which concern the New Testament; and to three ladies who produced a typescript from an often difficult manuscript; Mrs Janet Gillard, Mrs Iris Wheeler, and Mrs E. O. Wigginton.

1

Introduction:

God's story and God's word

The Bible is more a shelf of books than merely one volume: it is a collection of sixty-six compositions, of very varied size, covering a thousand years and more. They were written in Palestine, further east, and around the Mediterranean, and they use three languages, Hebrew (for most of them), Aramaic, a sister-language of Hebrew (for some chapters of Ezra and Daniel), and Greek (for the latest of the books).

The Hebrew and Aramaic books are called by the Jews 'the *Torah*, the Prophets, and the Writings'; to a Jew these are 'the scriptures'. Christians refer to them as the 'Old Testament' because they add to them the 'New Testament', the books written in Greek (though also written by Jews). Christianity places most emphasis on these later books, and often uses them to provide the key to understanding the earlier writings.

In this book, after three introductory chapters, we are going to look at the Bible mainly as 'God's story' and as 'God's word'. We begin with the story that starts with creation and takes the people of God down to the end of their independent political existence in 587 BC (chapters 4 and 5). Then we look at a retold version of the story which centres its interest in Israel's worship (chapter 6) and at some shorter stories (chapter 7) before coming to what Christians see as the climax of the story in Jesus of Nazareth (chapter 8).

Other parts of the Bible do not have the narrative form of the story: rather, they explicitly teach or preach. Thus we look in successive chapters at law, prophecy, wisdom, letter-writing, and visions (chapters 9–13). Then, after two chapters considering Israel's response in the form of her worship and her intellectual wrestling (chapters 14–15) we ask the question, How can the Bible speak today? (chapter 16).

The books collected into the Old and New Testaments are not the only old Jewish and Christian writings we have, and a case could be made for considering others as well as those treated here, which are the ones included in Protestant Bibles. The Bible as read by Catholic and Orthodox Christians includes some of the other Jewish writings, the 'apocrypha'. These belong to the period from the time of the latest Old Testament books up to that of the New Testament. They provide more examples of the kind of writings we look at here: further accounts of the story of the nation and further short stories (Tobit, Judith, Maccabees, 1 Esdras), as well as additions to the earlier stories and further visions (2 Esdras), two more wisdom books (Wisdom and Ecclesiasticus), and a further 'psalm' (the Prayer of Manasseh). Baruch is more difficult to classify: it has affinities with story, prophecy, psalmody, and wisdom.

A major reason for not going beyond the Old and New Testaments in this book, however, is that I have linked it to the *Good News Bible* which includes only the Old and New Testaments. Quotations come from GNB (as I shall refer to it) and I shall assume that the reader possesses a copy. So I have not generally repeated here information that GNB itself includes: for instance, in its introductions to each book, in its maps, and in its appendices. However, if you do not possess a *Good News Bible*, but are reading some other version, this book will still be of use to you.

Much of this book reflects not just my own reading of the Bible, but my reading of books about the Bible. This means that I am much indebted to other writers whom I have not specifically acknowledged. Where the experts disagree (as they often do) about historical questions, for instance, I have generally presented views that would be accepted by a majority of scholars; but anyone who reads further will find that often the questions are more complicated than the impression given by this introductory book!

The reader who wants to go further might try next:

S. Y. Blanch *For All Mankind* (Bible Reading Fellowship and John Murray)
S. Y. Blanch *The World Our Orphanage* (Epworth Press)
The Lion Handbook to the Bible (Lion Publishing)
B. W. Anderson *The Living World of the Old Testament* (Longman)
R. H. Gundry *A Survey of the New Testament* (Zondervan)

As a Christian I believe that the Bible is in a special sense God's book. By this I mean that God was behind its being written and that it tells me the truth about him and about ourselves.

But I believe it is also a human book. When God first created the world, he did it without human help. He said 'let there be light' – and there was light. He could have created the Bible the same way, no doubt. It could have dropped straight from heaven. But in fact it was written by human beings – men like Isaiah and Matthew. God worked through them and spoke to them. But the books are their work too.

The Bible is both God's book and man's book. So if we want to understand it, we will need a sympathy both for the God behind it and for the men behind it. You do not have to believe in God to be able to understand the Bible. But you do have to be sympathetic to the way it talks about God and about the world as his world. You have to have an open mind. You have to try to look at life the way it does, if you are to understand it.

You also have to have a sympathy for the men behind it. You are not a farmer in Hebron in 800 BC, or a scribe in Babylon in 400 BC, or a slave in Rome in AD 50. But you have to try to imagine how life was for them, if you are to understand the books they wrote or the books they read. And this is where we will begin.

2

The events of the Bible

THE ORIGINS OF ISRAEL (?2000–1200 BC)

The first date we can be reasonably sure of in the Bible is that of the Israelite people's escape from labour camps in Egypt under the leadership of Moses. The time is about 1275 BC. But the Israelites regarded the beginning of their story as the journey of Abraham and his family from Mesopotamia. Mesopotamia means 'between the rivers' and it denotes the country between the Rivers Tigris and Euphrates, 1000 km east of Palestine. It corresponds to the modern state of Iran (Persia) stretching down to the Persian Gulf.

One of the oldest and most splendid cities of Mesopotamia was 'Ur of the Chaldees'. Chaldea is another word for Babylonia, the later name of the country. For reasons we do not know – except that it was the Lord's call – a man named Nahor, with his wives and family, left Ur and travelled northwest to the town of Haran. After staying there a while the family, now headed by Abraham, in turn left Haran, and this time migrated in a south-westerly direction towards the land of the Canaanites.

Racially, Abraham's clan and the inhabitants of Canaan were related; their languages, too, were similar. They would be quite able to communicate with one another. But their cultures and ways of life were very different. The Canaanites were a settled, agricultural people. They worshipped a God named El, who had shrines throughout the land. Abraham's clan were shepherds, not farmers, and were thus less used to staying in one place: they might wander as they wished, and indeed were obliged to wander to some extent, ever in search of new pasturage for their flocks. Their God guided the leader of the clan – he was thus often called by the name of the leader, 'the God of Abraham', etc. – and accompanied them on their travels.

So Abraham and Sarah, Isaac and Rebecca, Jacob and Rachel and their twelve sons settled in Canaan. 'Settled' is a misleading word: they remained basically shepherds who would stay for a time in one place, but wander widely from this base.

They might have carried on living like this had it not been for a desperate famine which took Abraham's great-grandchildren to Egypt. There in fact they settled and lived happily, until there was a change of government and a king (or pharaoh) came to the throne who was not so sympathetic to these aliens in his country.

So by about 1300 the descendants of Jacob – whose other name was Israel – were no better than slaves of the Egyptians. At this time there were various Semite groups in Egypt, many of whom were put to work on building projects in the Delta area. But one group escaped, led by Moses. They raced east towards the Sinai peninsula and after a miraculous escape near the site of the present Suez Canal found refuge in the desert. It was an area Moses knew well, and he led them to the mountain where the God of Abraham had once appeared to him. There a pact was made between God and this people 'Israel'.

The pact is usually referred to in the Bible as a 'covenant'. The word denotes a solemn agreement made between two human beings, or between God and man, by which two parties promise to be faithful to one another for life. God had proved himself to them, and now they committed themselves to him. The 'ten commandments' and the other laws are the standard Israel agreed to accept as their part in keeping the covenant.

On leaving Sinai the Israelites lived as nomads for a generation, mostly in the northern part of the Sinai peninsula. Eventually the main body of them travelled up the east side of the Jordan rift, through the countries of Edom and Moab, and crossed the River Jordan near Jericho. It was these tribes' spectacular victories in the heart of the land that impressed themselves on later generations: the conquest under Joshua was the key to the Israelites' conquest of the land of Canaan. But before

Joshua's victories the land east of the Jordan was conquered separately, and the territory which became Judah was apparently attacked from the south by Caleb. Even in the centre and north some of the peoples of Canaan accepted the invaders, without resistance, perhaps recognizing them as their own kin and acknowledging the invaders' God as their own too. One way and another Israel could claim possession of the hill country west of the Jordan and of a fair slice of territory the other side.

The following parts of the Bible refer to these events:

Israel's ancestors	Genesis (Job is also set in this period)
The exodus	Exodus 1–15
The covenant at Sinai	Exodus 16–40; Leviticus; Numbers 1–10
The time of wandering	Numbers 11–36; Deuteronomy
The conquest under Joshua	Joshua

CHAOS AND KINGSHIP (1200–931)

The story of the conquest ought to lead into 'and lived happily ever after'. In fact it is only the beginning of Israel's troubles. Many Canaanite clans had not been defeated by the Israelites; even the later capital, Jerusalem, was still controlled by the Jebusites. Furthermore, at about the same time as the Israelites were making inroads on Canaanite territory from the east, the Philistines – who came originally from across the Mediterranean – were doing the same from the west. While the Canaanites might be doomed by this pincer movement, it was not clear that Israel would be the eventual victors.

But the Canaanites themselves formed an even more serious threat to Israel in another way. Their religion had a beguiling attraction for the Israelites. The Israelites' God, Yahweh, or Jehovah*, had proved himself able to meet his people's needs in rescuing her from oppression and aiding her in battle. But

* GNB and most other English Bibles translate this as 'The LORD'.

could he make crops grow? There might be doubt about that. On the other hand, making crops grow was the speciality of the Canaanite god Baal (El's son) – so his worshippers claimed. And often Israelites fell to the temptation to join in his worship. Moral chaos characterized these early years in Palestine, too: 'everyone did just as he pleased' (Judges 21. 25).

Renowned leaders such as Deborah, Gideon, Samson, and Samuel belong to this period. They were the 'judges' – the title is misleading, for they were primarily figures through whom God rescued his people from apostasy and oppression. But the Israelites never won final security, and (with the Philistine threat increasing and Samuel now old), they eventually insisted on having the organized leadership required by the challenge of the situation: on having kings, like everyone else.

The first king was Saul, a man who won notable victories, though without being able to deal with the Philistine threat. Nor did he deal with the problem of religious anarchy: indeed he contributed to the problem by his own falling away from Yahwism and his final recourse to the medium of Endor. He died in battle with the Philistines.

Even in his lifetime a younger man named David, a southerner (unlike Saul), had been cutting a more impressive figure. He was soon made king over the southern clans and eventually, when the family and followers of Saul were eliminated, over the northern tribes too.

David was a key figure in Israel's history. He disposed of the Philistine threat and in fact created an empire that for his lifetime dominated the area both sides of the Jordan. He captured Jerusalem, and there he installed 'the covenant box' – a symbol of Yahweh's presence that went back to the time at Sinai. His innovations mark a significant stage in the development of Israel's worship, and in particular the musical tradition of the temple (especially psalmody) is traced back to him – though the building of the temple was not to be put into effect in his lifetime.

In the area of personal relations, however, he was weak, and in particular he never properly handled the key question of who was to be his successor. Eventually Solomon emerged. His achievement was the actual building of the temple. He is also credited with the originating of the teaching of 'wisdom' in Israel, particularly as this is represented in the advice on everyday life offered by Proverbs; and the cultural development that belongs to his reign may have included the writing of the first connected history in Israel. But he was unable to do more than hang on precariously to the Davidic empire. In his reign the weaknesses that were to destroy the state became clear.

The following parts of the Bible refer to this period:

The Judges and Saul	Judges; 1 Samuel
David	2 Samuel; 1 Chronicles; Psalms
Solomon	1 Kings 1–11; 2 Chronicles 1–9; Proverbs

DECLINE AND FALL (931–587)

Solomon was a statesman, and that was part of his undoing (he was willing to compromise over questions of faith in 'the national interest'). His son Rehoboam was not a statesman, and that was his undoing.

We have noted that conditions in Palestine had militated against the tribes really being one nation until they were united by a king. Now that fragile unity disintegrated, and Rehoboam lost the allegiance of virtually all the tribes except his own, Judah. Thus from now on there were two independent states, Judah (ruled by a descendant of David) and to her north the main body of the tribes who inherited the title 'Israel'. Jerusalem remained in Judah; it was now at the extreme northern end of the kingdom. The kings of Judah and of Israel are listed below (pp. 18–19).

The story of Israel is short and bloody. Its first king, Jeroboam, made an astute midwife for the new state, though he is condemned for establishing shrines to replace Jerusalem in his people's affections. His son Nadab was assassinated and succeeded by one Baasha. His son Elah was also assassinated and succeeded by one of his generals, Zimri, who was in turn soon overthrown in another coup and replaced by the army chief-of-staff, Omri.

Omri was the greatest of Israel's kings; he was responsible for the building of its permanent capital, Samaria. His son Ahab, who married the infamous Jezebel, was hounded by the first great prophet known to us, Elijah, on account of both the religious and the social enormities that increasingly characterized Israel. The lifetimes of Elijah and his successor, Elisha, also saw the beginning of external troubles for Israel in the attacks by the Syrians and other smaller nations, during the time of Ahab and his sons Ahaziah and Jehoram (Joram). Elisha then instigated another army coup; one of the generals, Jehu, elminated Jehoram, his mother, and the rest of Ahab's family, and reformed Israel's religion. Jehu's descendants Jehoahaz, Jehoash (Joash), another Jeroboam, and Zechariah made his line the longest to last in Israel, but it was finally ended when Zechariah was assassinated by Shallum – who was then shortly removed by Menahem.

Menahem's reign sees the death-knell begin to ring for Israel. The Assyrians, who had created an empire in Mesopotamia, began to turn their mind to the west. Israel became their vassal. Menahem's son Pekahiah was killed by a general Pekah, and Pekah by Hoshea. During their century the first prophets to have books named after them, Amos and Hosea (see pp. 104–5) began to warn Israel that continuing religious apostasy and social unrighteousness would bring judgement. But the message was not heeded and in 722 Samaria fell to the Assyrians. The Israelites were deported and their land settled by peoples who had been the victims of Assyrian conquest elsewhere. The northern tribes virtually ceased to exist.

During this tumultuous history of the northern kingdom, the history of Judah was internally and externally much less eventful. The line of David held the throne till the end of the state's existence, even after the assassination of individuals in that line such as Joash and his son Amaziah. Judah was weaker than Israel, and was often under pressure from her big brother to the north. Another note that recurs in her story is the question of how far she was faithful to Yahweh, and how far the kings

THE HISTORY OF ISRAEL AND JUDAH

				Israel	Judah	
			Jeroboam I	931	931	Rehoboam
					913	Abijam (Abijah)
			Nadab	910	911	Asa
			Baasha	909		
900			Elah	886		
			Zimri	885		
			Tibni	885		
			Omri	885	870	Jehoshaphat
			Ahab	874		
	(Syrians	ELIJAH				
	invading		Ahaziah	853		
	Israel)	ELISHA	Jehoram	852	848	Jehoram
			Jehu	841	841	Ahaziah
					841	Athaliah
					835	Jehoash (Joash)
			Jehoahaz	814		
800			Jehoash	798	796	Amaziah
			Jeroboam II	782		
					781	Azariah (Uzziah)
		AMOS				
		HOSEA				

		Zechariah	743				
		Shallum	743				
		Menahem	743				
		Pekahiah	738	740	Jotham	ISAIAH	(Assyrians threatening Judah)
	(Assyrians threatening Israel)	Pekah	737	736	Ahaz	MICAH	
		Hoshea	732				
	Assyria puts an end to Israel		722				
700				716	Hezekiah		
						ISAIAH	
				687	Manasseh		
				642	Amon	NAHUM	
				640	Josiah	ZEPHANIAH	
						JEREMIAH	
				609	Jehoahaz (Joahaz)		(Babylonians put an end to Assyria, threaten Judah)
				609	Jehoiakim		
						HABAKKUK	
600				598	Jehoiachin	(Babylonians take Jerusalem)	
				598	Zedekiah	JEREMIAH, EZEKIEL	
				587	Babylonians take Jerusalem again		

failed to walk in David's ways. But even in this matter she proved less susceptible than Israel to being led astray. Judah was more isolated (by the steepness of her mountain slopes, for instance), more cut off from the likely mainstream of history. Israel fell first partly because her position exposed her to greater pressure.

The rise of Assyria and the appearance of the classical prophets affected Judah too, however. Isaiah (see pp. 92–7) declared that Assyria was a greater threat to her than Syria and Israel, and in the time of Hezekiah Judah did almost fall to the Assyrians. Hezekiah's successor Manasseh is regarded as the lowest apostate who ever occupied Judah's throne, and the effects of his policies could not be eradicated even by the great reformer Josiah who followed him. The end of the sixth century saw Assyria herself fall. Judah's next overlord was Babylon, whom she failed to take seriously enough, and in 587, after serious warnings, the Babylonians devastated Jerusalem and introduced direct rule.

The following parts of the Bible refer to this period:
1 Kings 12–2 Kings 25
2 Chronicles 10–36
Amos, Hosea, Isaiah 1–39, Micah
Nahum, Zephaniah, Habakkuk, Jeremiah

VASSAL OF BABYLON AND PERSIA (587–333)

The exiles of Judah were fortunate as the exiles of Israel had not been. Babylonian policy was to remove only the leaders of troublesome nations, not to transport whole peoples. The Judaean politicians, princes, and priests were in fact able to lead a tolerable life in Babylon. Indeed in some ways the bulk of the ordinary population, left behind leaderless in the devastated land of Judah, were actually less fortunate. The five poems in Lamentations (see p. 136) give us some idea of their feelings. Many people left Judah voluntarily; the process of spreading the Jews all over the world had begun. Eventually the worship of the synagogue – concentrating on prayer and the reading of the scriptures – developed, probably initially in Babylon. This helped to make up for separation from the temple, and played an important part in keeping the people of Israel in being when they were not in their own land.

The books of Kings were compiled at the time of the exile, and by telling the story of Israel's and Judah's sin they comprise an acknowledgement that the exile had to happen. But even before the catastrophe itself, prophets such as Jeremiah (in Jerusalem, see pp. 97–101) and Ezekiel (already transported to Babylon in 597, see pp. 102–4) had been promising that, although the crisis had to be undergone and a long exile experienced, there would be a return to the land. The signal that this day was imminent was the growth of the Persian empire under Cyrus, referred to in Isaiah 45. Cyrus put an end to the Babylonian empire and allowed the various captives there – including the people of Judah – to resume their own religion and return home.

Apparently the Jews were in no hurry to go back to far off, primitive Palestine; but some did so. The temple in Jerusalem was rebuilt by Zerubbabel, a descendant of David who did not, however, occupy the throne to which he was heir. In fact Judah never had her own kings again. Apparently prophecy, too, disappeared soon after the time of Haggai and Zechariah (see pp. 106–7), Zerubbabel's contemporaries, whose messages reflect how hard life was in the years after the return from exile. The priests and, later, the scribes became the leaders of the post-exilic community, which was ruled by the word of the law.

The Jews wrote no connected history of the Persian era, and we know for certain only about one part of this period, the activities of Ezra and Nehemiah, who came from the exile in the middle of the fifth century. Ezra was commissioned by the Persian king to see that religious matters were being conducted in the proper way in Jerusalem, and this commission led to his initiating various reforms there. Nehemiah's activity overlapped with Ezra's. His visit to Jerusalem was prompted by news that the devastation of the previous century had not yet been repaired. He was responsible for rebuilding the defences of the city, as well as for social and religious reforms.

Predictably, the rebuilding of the walls aroused the opposition of other peoples living in the area, and tension between the Judaeans and related groups is a feature of this period. In particular an animosity developed between Jews and Samaritans (see p. 30).

The attitudes of the Jewish people in the post-exilic period can be inferred from the writings of this time. If we do not have the names of notable prophets after Malachi, nevertheless many treasured the message of the prophets and longed for the time when God would again act in history and bring the triumph of his people. Other Jews found it hard to make sense of the old faith, and Job and Qoheleth (Ecclesiastes) (see pp. 141–8) reflect their doubts and uncertainties. Others again, however, tried hard to see what God was doing and what he required. One work that belongs to this period is the books of Chronicles (see pp. 60–64), with their interest in the temple and its services: the worship of the people of God is clearly regarded as very important. The final editing of the first five books of the Bible, the 'pentateuch', also belongs here, and a delight in God's law and a concern to obey him in every detail of life also characterize the years after the exile.

The following parts of the Bible refer to this period:
Lamentations
Ezekiel, Isaiah 40–66, Daniel
Haggai, Zechariah, Malachi
Ezra–Nehemiah

PROVINCE OF GREECE AND ROME (333 BC–AD 135)

The rule of the Persians was ended by the triumph of the Greeks under Alexander the Great. In 332 Alexander passed through Palestine on his way to Egypt; Judaea probably escaped actual invasion, again because of its out-of-the-way position.

Alexander's empire lasted only a decade. In 323 he died, and his generals fought over his empire. The area north of Palestine was then ruled by Seleucus and his descendants; Egypt, to the south, was controlled by the Ptolemies. Palestine again found itself a buffer state.

We have noted that earlier rulers attempted to crush the national aspirations of conquered peoples by transportation, while the Persians encouraged a positive attitude to their rule by their support of people's religious idiosyncrasies (provided these were harmless). The Greeks brought a culture that influenced their empire more than the Babylonians or Persians ever did. Jews in Alexandria in Egypt, a very Hellenistic city, translated their Bible into Greek (the Septuagint) and began actually to write in Greek. Many of these Greek books were included in some versions of the Christian Bible (they are referred to by Protestants as the 'apocrypha').

But the centre of Judaism remained the temple in Jerusalem, and there Judaism found itself involved in a fight for its life with Hellenism. In 198 Palestine had passed from Ptolemaic to Seleucid control, and the Seleucid king Antiochus Epiphanes (175–163) sought to unite his empire by imposing Greek religion and culture on all his subject peoples. He banned the Jewish religion and had the Jerusalem temple turned into a shrine to Zeus – the original 'awful horror' referred to in the book of Daniel (11.31). This provoked at first passive resistance and then armed revolt among some Jews. These rebels, called the 'Maccabees', proved too much for the Seleucids, who never regained control of Palestine. As Daniel promised (8.25), the 'little horn', Antiochus, was broken.

The pressures of Hellenization led some groups to set up an alternative society. The most notable of these was the Qumran community, who established a religious foundation on the shores of the Dead Sea. The Pharisees sought to remain faithful to the law without withdrawing from Jerusalem. The Sadducees proved more adaptable and held power in the temple.

The decline of the Seleucids was accompanied by the increasing power of the Romans. Eventually the Romans sent Pompey the Great to secure the eastern boundary of their empire, and in 63 BC he arrived in Jerusalem, ended the rule of the descendants of the Maccabees, and made Judaea part of the Roman province of Syria.

The Romans established a puppet-monarchy in Palestine, the house of Herod. Herod 'the Great' enlarged and rebuilt the temple and undertook other building projects in Jerusalem and elsewhere – including the creation of the new seaport of Caesarea (named after the emperor).

After Herod the Great's death there was rebellion against Rome. None of his family were as capable as he, and eventually his kingdom was divided, with Herodian 'tetrarchs' in charge in the north, and Judaea under the direct rule of Roman governors. Many Jews were hopeful that their God might intervene, but not many of them accepted the claims of any of the 'messiahs' of the time. The most important of these messianic figures, Jesus of Nazareth, was executed during the governorship of Pontius Pilate. Subsequently his followers continued to propagate a belief that nevertheless he was the messiah, and both Jewish and Roman authorities found the followers of Jesus difficult to handle.

For the most part the Roman empire was a support rather than a hindrance to the Jewish faith, and there were Jewish communities – some of whose members were of Jewish birth, some converts – all round the Mediterranean. The stability of the Roman empire and the spread of these Jewish communities made it easier for the followers of Jesus to spread the belief that he was the messiah through the eastern Mediterranean and beyond – though most of the converts were actually gentiles. The key figure in this achievement was a converted Jew from Tarsus, Saul or Paul. The Christian correspondence which has survived in the New Testament, as well as the book of Acts, indicates that these Christian communities were spread through Turkey, Greece, and as far as Rome itself.

In Palestine, however, relations between Jews and Romans deteriorated. The Jews rebelled in AD 66, and Jerusalem and its temple were destroyed in AD 70. The next century saw a further rebellion, quelled in AD 135, when Jerusalem was made a Roman city from which the Jews were banned.

The following parts of the Bible refer to this period:
Daniel
The New Testament
(The Old Testament apocrypha belongs here.)

3

The land of the Bible

Three very different areas form the scene of the Bible story. It begins in the powerful empires of Mesopotamia (modern Iran) and Egypt. The flat plains of Mesopotamia are the background of the story of the Garden of Eden, of the Flood, of the Tower of Babylon, and of the call of Abraham. It was to Babylon that many leading Jews were exiled in 597 and 587 BC, and Babylon was from then on an important centre of Judaism. Babylon is also a symbol of oppression. So is Egypt: in fact, the chief importance of the land of the Nile is as the land of affliction from which the Israelites were rescued in the time of Moses. It, too, was a place of exile from 587 and a centre of subsequent Judaism.

Egypt belongs also to the very different area where the Bible story ends, in the west, as the message of Christianity is passed on to Turkey, Greece, Italy and Spain. The feature of this area that distinguishes it from the east is that it centres on the sea. It was largely by sea, across the Mediterranean, that the Christian message spread. These countries also belonged to the empire of the Romans, the most important political feature of the period. Rome, like Babylon and Egypt, is a symbol of oppression in the New Testament.

The Bible story really centres, however, on a third area, 'the holy land' which lies between the empires of Mesopotamia, of the Nile, and of the Mediterranean. Somehow this land has always been a cockpit of history, a buffer zone between major powers, without ever being the centre of a major empire itself (except perhaps in the time of David and Solomon). Perhaps its position at the junction of the continents of Asia, Europe, and

Africa contributes to its being a meeting-point of peoples and their history.

The boundaries of this land often changed, as do the boundaries of modern states. The name changed too. Before the Israelites came, it was the land of Canaan, and later it was named Palestine (after the Philistines). Since Israel is the name of a particular state today, and Palestine may become the name of another one, in this section we will use the old name Canaan as the name of the land in which the Jews lived.

Canaan is a small country. The area spoken of in the Bible includes parts of what is now Lebanon (the area of Tyre and Sidon), of Syria (the Golan) and of Jordan (Gilead, east of the Jordan, and the whole of the 'West Bank', including many of the most important towns of the Bible – Shechem, Samaria, the old city of Jerusalem, Bethlehem, and Hebron), as well as the State of Israel. Nevertheless, from Dan to Beersheba (Israel's equivalent of Maine to Florida) is only 250 km. East to west, the land measures 80 to 120 km. Jerusalem is only 60 km or so from either Tel Aviv or Amman.

But within this small country there is amazing variation. There are fertile plains on the coast and in Jezreel, but steep mountains inland, like the Atlantic coastal plain and the Appalachian Mountains. Between the mountains of Israel and Lebanon, and those of Jordan and Syria, is the valley of the River Jordan, in the north shallow and rich, to the south steep and dry (except for oases such as Jericho). There is a mountain range which rises to 2,800 m and a valley which contains the lowest lying sea on earth; and there is at the same time snow on the former and, a few miles away, sun-baked desert around the latter. There are dry river-beds which in winter briefly become raging torrents, and scorched hills which in spring become carpeted with flowers.

Canaan may be divided into four vertical stripes – the plains, the mountains west of the Jordan, the Jordan valley, and the mountains east of the Jordan. Each of them becomes higher the further you travel north, drier and less cultivable the further you travel south.

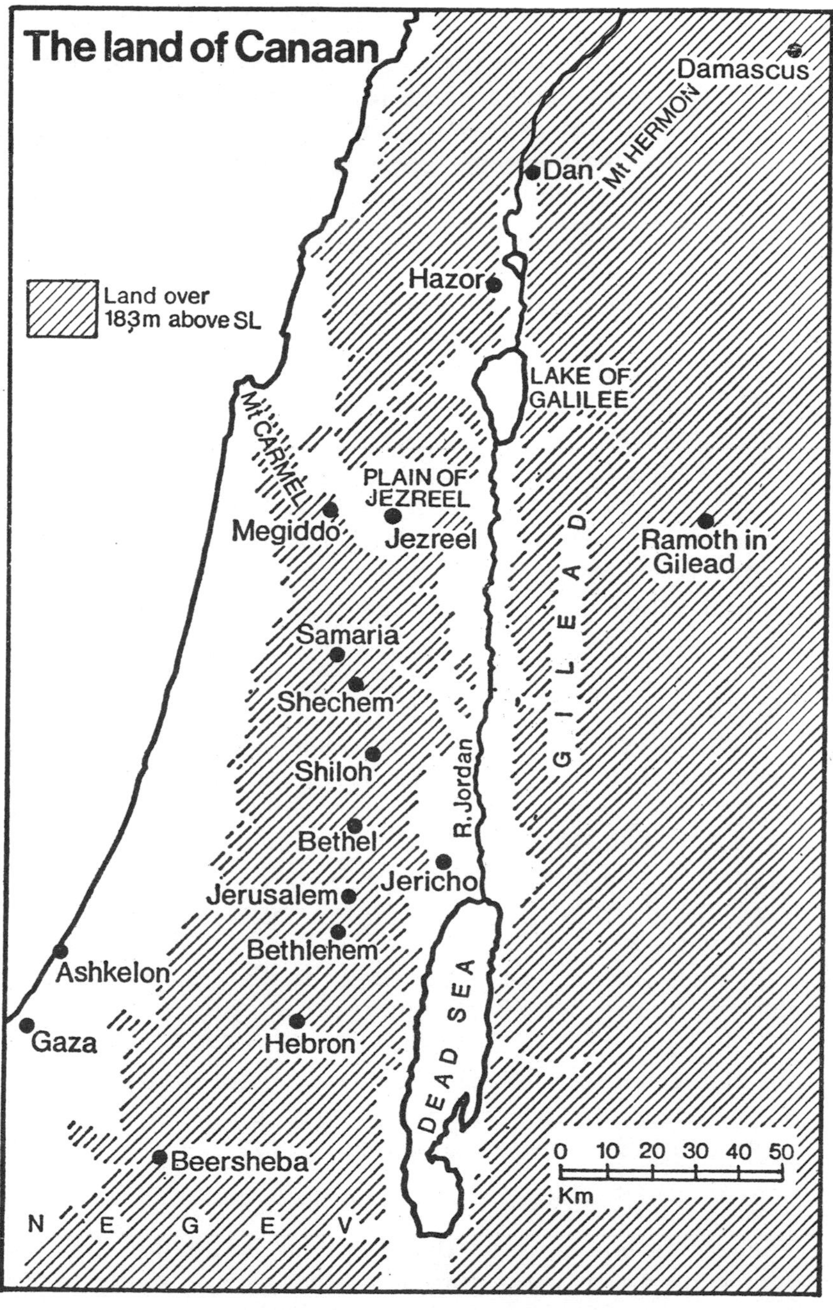
The land of Canaan
Land over 183m above SL
Damascus
Mt HERMON
Dan
Hazor
LAKE OF GALILEE
Mt CARMEL
PLAIN OF JEZREEL
Megiddo
Jezreel
GILEAD
Ramoth in Gilead
Samaria
Shechem
Shiloh
R. Jordan
Bethel
Jericho
Jerusalem
Bethlehem
Ashkelon
Gaza
Hebron
DEAD SEA
Beersheba
0 10 20 30 40 50
Km
N E G E V

THE PLAINS

For practical purposes, the most important parts of this land are probably the plains, which form a strip along the coast and then from the Bay of Haifa drive a wedge inland (the plain of Jezreel). Most of the main roads (and railways) have generally run along these plains. Much of the most fertile land is here, and fruit, cotton, and other crops are grown (though some of the land was marshy until recently). But in the south, where the coastal plain is broadest and curves round the south of the mountains, it becomes desert – 'the Negev'. Beersheba, a centre as important in the time of Abraham as today, dominates this steppe area.

Many of the states that have controlled Canaan were centred on the plains. In pre- and early-Israelite times the great cities of the Canaanites and the Philistines were here (Beth-Shean, Megiddo, Gezer, Ashkelon, Gaza, etc.). The Romans built Caesarea on the coast by the plain, and modern times have seen substantial urban growth here, especially around Tel Aviv and Haifa. It has always been the more sophisticated nation that controlled the plain: the less advanced had to make do with the mountains.

The plain of Jezreel is the great battleground of the Bible – the scene of the victories of Deborah and Barak over the Canaanites (Judges 4) and Gideon over the Midianites (Judges 11), the scene of the deaths of Saul at the hand of the Philistines (1 Samuel 32) and Josiah at the hand of the Egyptians (2 Kings 23), the scene of the last battle to come at 'Armageddon' (mountain of Megiddo).

In the southern half of the land the plain is separated from the mountains by hills like those in upstate New York—the 'hill country' or 'lowlands' in the Old Testament. This formed a natural first line of defence for Judah especially against the Philistines, and it was the scene of exploits on the part of Joshua, Samson, and David.

ACROSS THE JORDAN

The eastern boundary of 'the holy land' is the mountain chain which rises east of the Jordan and which eventually becomes the Arabian desert. In the far north is Mount Hermon, whose snow-capped peak dwarfs all the mountains of the holy land itself into mere hillocks. To its south, and to the east and south-east of Lake Galilee, are the lands of Bashan and Gilead, once evidently a prosperous area (its cattle were renowned), but recently notorious as a theatre of war (Bashan is the 'Golan heights'). In New Testament times the area of Gilead was predominantly Greek and it was called by the Greek name Decapolis ('ten cities'); Jesus journeyed there.

Across the Golan heights runs a road from Damascus and the north and east, to Lake Galilee and the south. This road marks the route of the patriarchs (the fords of the Jordan are named after Jacob's daughters), of the Jews going into exile and returning, and of the journey of Saul to Damascus. It was on the way down from the Golan heights that Saul was confronted by the Lord (Acts 9).

Gilead and the plateau to the south (known as Ammon, then Moab, then Edom or Idumaea) belong today to the State of Jordan. These peoples were defeated by the Israelites under Moses on the way to Canaan after the exodus (Numbers 20), and again at the time of Israel's greatest power by David (2 Samuel 10). But they often formed a thorn in Israel's flesh.

WEST OF THE JORDAN

The centre of attention in the Bible lies not in these two outer stripes, however, but primarily in the mountains west of the Jordan: Galilee, Samaria, and Judaea.

Galilee in the north is mentioned rarely in the Old Testament. But it features in the New Testament as the home of Jesus and the scene of much of his ministry. The mountains here rise steeply from the Mediterranean on the west and from Lake Galilee in the east – though there is no shortage of feasible east-west routes across these mountains. The lake itself takes its name from the area, rather than the other way round, and 'Galilee' in the Bible (and today) refers more often to the whole area itself than to the lake to the east. The best known town in Galilee today is Nazareth; but in New Testament times this was an insignificant hamlet. Safed, too, the most important Jewish town in modern Galilee, has become important only in relatively recent times.

Galilee is a fertile area. A proverb says that it is easier to raise a legion of olives in Galilee than to bring up a child in Palestine. Wheat and grapes abound also. Further north, the hills of Galilee become the mountains of Lebanon, with their famous cedar forests that provided the timber for Solomon's temple.

Samaria, the centre of the land, includes the towns of Shechem, Shiloh, Bethel, and modern Ramallah, as well as Omri's city of Samaria which gave the area its name. All these cities lay on or near the ridge of the mountains which form one range, the spine of the country as a whole, falling away to the east and west. They slope fairly gently, however, and there are several reasonably easy access routes from the plain into the mountains – especially to Shechem (modern Nablus, the capital of the West Bank), which also has an easy route east to the Jordan and thus marks an important cross roads. Shechem was Abraham's first stopping point (Genesis 12), the site of Jacob's well (and there of the meeting of Jesus and the Samaritan woman in John 4), the site of the reading of the covenant law and of the remaking of the covenant in the time of Joshua (chapter 24).

To the north, the mountains include a spur which runs north-west until it tumbles into the Mediterranean Sea at Haifa and causes the only hiccup on the straight line of coast from Lebanon to Egypt. This north-western spur is Mount Carmel, the scene of Elijah's contest with the Baal prophets (1 Kings 18). Most north-south traffic along the plains crosses the mountains just south-east of Mount Carmel at the strategic pass guarded on the Jezreel side by Megiddo.

Samaria and Galilee belonged to the northern tribes of Israel, dominated by Ephraim. These tribes went independent of the south after the death of Solomon, and they also modified the old religion. In 722 they were conquered by the Assyrians and many of their population were replaced by foreigners. Thus 'Samaritan' came to mean religiously and racially impure. The Samaritans were half-way to being gentiles. Similarly Galilee, which had never been effectively conquered, became known as 'Galilee of the Gentiles' (Isaiah 9.1). It was the far north, provincial and outcast.

Judaea and Samaria correspond broadly to the 'West Bank', the area of Canaan west of the River Jordan which became part of the State of Jordan in 1947 and was occupied by the State of Israel in 1967. The ridge of mountains continues southwards without any very perceptible break as Samaria ceases and Judaea (Judah) begins. The line of familiar locations continues – Jerusalem, Bethlehem, Hebron – and these towns, with the ones listed above, are the places on the journeys of Abraham and his successors up and down Palestine, and on the route taken by Joseph, Mary and Jesus between Nazareth, Jerusalem, Bethlehem, and the south (when the family sought refuge in Egypt).

If anything distinguishes Judaea from Samaria, it is that Judaea (as we noted in chapter 2) is more isolated. The slopes to the east and west are steeper and there are no significant cross routes south of Jerusalem because on the east there is nothing to cross to – only the Dead Sea. Yet although the eastern part of Judaea is quite inhospitable (it was here that Bishop Pike met his death a few years ago, only a handful of miles from civilization), the ridge itself and the western slopes of the mountains are well-watered. They still produce an abundance of grapes, and the giant bunch found here by Moses' spies, Joshua and Caleb (Numbers 13), is now the symbol of the Israeli Government Tourist Office.

THE JORDAN

The final stripe of country we need to describe is the most extraordinary. The Jordan 'rift' is an extensive fault in the earth's surface – a crack which extends to nearly 400 m below sea level at the Dead Sea. Its beginning lies far north of Canaan, but it becomes important to us at the point where the headwaters of the Jordan emerge from the foothills of Hermon. Here, at the point where the modern states of Israel, Lebanon, and Syria meet, these full-grown streams gush from the mountains. The river is one of the very few that flow all year round, fed as it is by the snows that are still seeping through the mountain in high summer.

Near one of these streams is the Israelite town of Dan – like Bethel a religious centre of northern Israel. Near another is the famous Roman town of Caesarea Philippi, the scene of Jesus's recognition as messiah by Peter (Matthew 16). Probably the mountains here were also the scene of Jesus's 'transfiguration' before the disciples, which the gospels describe just after the Caesarea Philippi incident.

The broad Jordan valley rolls down, between the mountains of Galilee and the Golan, to Lake Galilee, passing the ancient Canaanite city of Hazor from which Jabin dominated the Galilee area till the Israelites arrived (Joshua 11). On the busy northern shore of the lake there were flourishing Jewish cities in the time of Jesus – Chorazim, Capernaum, Bethsaida. But they were destroyed (as he said they would be) soon after his time. As you travel down the western side of the lake you pass the scenes of Jesus's ministry and eventually the Greek city of Tiberias.

The lake itself is harp-shaped, 20 km long and 12 km wide. It is below sea level, and the climate is humid. It is noteworthy that the New Testament makes no reference to the climate of this area which is so important to its story. (The Old Testament does refer sometimes to climate: for instance in its references to the sun, with its dangers, and to flash floods, which can bring an unexpected victory.) Perhaps in the humid summer months people relaxed and avoided long journeys.

South of the lake the waters become the river again and meander south through a narrower valley. Near the water itself there is the thick growth referred to as 'jungle' in the Bible. But as the level of the land falls steadily the surroundings become drier. The area illustrates the statement that a tree with its roots down near a river can remain fruitful, but away from this source of water it withers (Psalm 1). For there is no rain left in the Mediterranean winds by the time they reach the Jordan side of the mountain ridge. It is this part of the river that was the scene of John the Baptist's ministry (Matthew 3), as it had been earlier where Elisha told Naaman to wash (2 Kings 5). The

Jordan flows into the Dead Sea near the oasis of Jericho (scene of Joshua's first famous victory and of Jesus's meetings with Zacchaeus and Bartimaeus, and the starting point of what was then a tortuous and dangerous road up to Jerusalem). The water never leaves this sea, except upwards by evaporation. But the minerals in the water do not evaporate; they accumulate to make the lake (80 km long) the Dead Sea, or 'the Salt Sea' as it is called in Hebrew. There are some wonderful fresh water oases in the area – Jericho, En Gedi – but for the most part it is a dead world. The valley, as it continues waterless to the south to the Gulf of Aqaba, is called the Arabah.

It is worth trying to get a feeling of the geography and climate of Canaan, because this often contributes to an understanding of the drift of the story.

T–HTRB–B

The story of God and his people

In the first section, I reviewed the Bible's history. Now we look at the Bible's story. What is the difference?

By the Bible's history I meant the actual, unadorned events which happened between 2000 BC and AD 100: the main features of a stream of happenings which was just one among many streams (the histories of the Egyptians, of the Greeks, of the British, and so on). I tried to describe these events as factually as possible, to note the political and social developments, to set the story on the wide canvas of the international events of the period. I avoided theology (there was little mention of God) and morals (I did not suggest that anyone ought not to have acted as he did). In this way, the history of the Jews or of the Christian Church can be written as factually as the history of the Arabs or of the British Labour Party – though in all these examples the biases of the writer and of his age will appear, of course!

However, such objective history is at no point what the Bible tries to give. In this sense, it is a mistake to treat the Bible as a history book.

Having said that, we must immediately add that it is a book of history in the sense that the story it relates is one that happened. It is not like Hans Andersen; it is not like a novel. Many of the events it records are also mentioned by other ancient writings. For instance, the Babylonians left their own account of the capture of Jerusalem; the Romans found cause to refer to Jesus of Nazareth.

The Bible itself emphasizes that the events in its story really happened. It was because their God did things that the Jews could know he was really God. It was because Jesus rose from the dead that his disciples challenged people to believe in him.

Nevertheless, the story in which the account of these events is given is not written as history is today. The writers are not interested in what was of mere 'historical' significance – in politics or culture or social developments for their own sake. They are interested in what God was doing with his people, in how people were responding to God, and in the lessons that this story has for their readers. They are concerned to communicate, to make the story interesting, to make it intelligible for the sake of later readers.

We keep wanting to ask the question, 'Did it really happen?' or rather, 'Did they really think it happened?' (if we know, or think we know, that it cannot have done). Did the serpent get on its hind legs and speak? Did the walls of Jericho fall? Did the whale swallow Jonah? Often it is impossible to answer these questions, and we must be content with a different approach. The writers claim that their story is basically historical. Having said that, they invite us to respond to it as it stands as a story, to see what it means and what it has to say.

So one key way by which the Bible writers communicated God's message to their day was by telling a story. This meant that the same story came to be retold several times, because new lessons needed to be drawn out of it. Thus there are four gospels in the New Testament, each with a different emphasis and message. There are two accounts of the history from David to the exile, in Samuel–Kings and Chronicles, two accounts written to bring different messages to different periods (the time of the exile itself, and the period after God's people had returned from exile).

There were probably also at least two accounts of the earlier story, from the creation to Moses, though these have now been combined into one in the first four books of the Bible. These books often seem to repeat themselves: for instance, we are twice told about the creation itself (Genesis 1 and 2), and twice God's revealing his name to Moses is described (Exodus 3 and 6). Probably these repetitions are the clues to the interweaving of two versions of the story – just as in Christian times there have been attempts to weave the four gospels into one, so that people can read 'the whole story' of Jesus in one book.

To some extent the threads which make up the books can be unwoven, and we can then see how the story was applied to the people of different periods. We will note some examples of this below. But it is a delicate exercise, and is ultimately speculative. Since only the conflated version has been preserved, it will be best to concentrate on that.

THE STORY OF GOD AND HIS PEOPLE: GENESIS TO KINGS

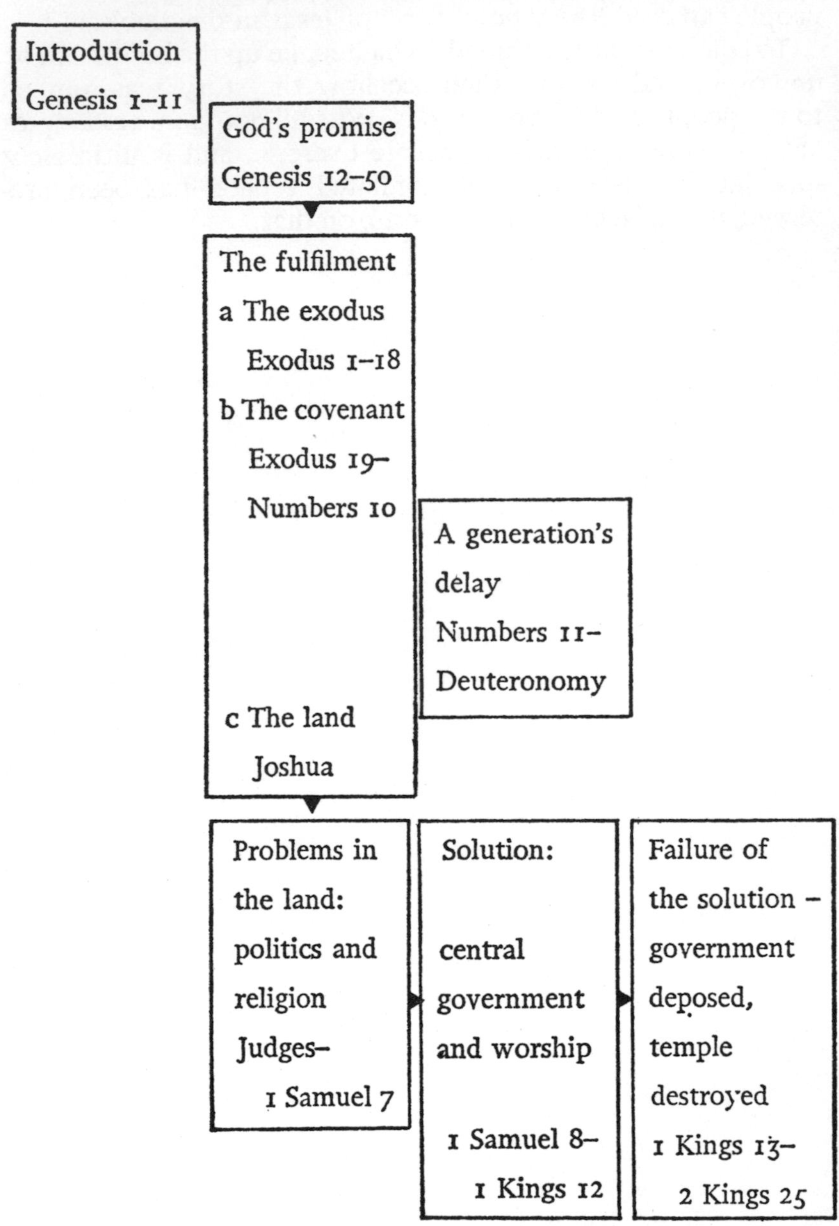

4

Beginnings:

Genesis to Numbers

The first five books of the Bible are 'the *torah*' (to Jews), 'the five books of Moses' (to Christians). They do not claim to have been written by Moses (titles such as 'the first book of Moses' in the old English translations are not part of the original text, and do not appear in Hebrew Bibles). But Moses does dominate them, and any reliable information they contain about the events related by Exodus to Deuteronomy (Moses does not appear in Genesis) must go back to him.

Torah is a Hebrew word which is often translated 'law'. But its meaning is broader: 'teaching' is perhaps the nearest English word. As well as law, it includes the story of how Israel came to be God's people, and how they came to the borders of the land of Canaan. Indeed, the narrative of God's dealings with the whole world, and in particular with Israel's ancestors, provides the framework for the opening books of the Bible. The actual laws came within the framework of the chart on the following page.

It is difficult to know where to place the end of the first stage in Israel's story. The *torah* sees the first *five* books together. As the chart on p. 40 suggests, however, the book of Joshua marks the point where God's keeping of his promises to Israel is brought to fulfilment: in a sense the first *six* books belong together. Deuteronomy and Joshua, however, look forward to the life in the promised land which is described in the books that come later (Samuel—Kings: see the diagram on p. 38) so in this chapter we will look at the first *four* books, Genesis to Numbers.

THE STORY OF MAN (Genesis 1–11)

The Bible begins (Genesis 1–11) by picturing God's creation of the world and of man. He gives Adam and Eve a garden to live in, but they are expelled when they ignore his word. Their descendants struggle to cope with life East of Eden but the situation deteriorates until God almost allows the world to be destroyed. After the flood disaster, it deteriorates again and God makes a further new start by calling a man named Abraham, the Israelites' ancestor, to follow him.

So the Bible starts with stories about the earliest history of the world and of man. This is actually rather surprising. No history of any other nation starts from the creation of the world – but this history of Israel does. The other ancient religions had stories about the creation, but they did not go on to link the story of creation to their own history. Ancient and modern man kept creation and history in two separate compartments. Israel links them firmly together.

We do not know when these creation stories were written down. The book of Genesis does not tell us who wrote it. But there are at least three situations to which Genesis as a whole seems to have a particular relevance.

Genesis 1–11	the beginnings of the world
Genesis 12–50	the beginnings of Israel: God's promises given
Exodus 1–19	Israel's deliverance from Egypt (some laws)
Exodus 20–40 Leviticus Numbers 1–10	**laws given at Sinai (some narrative)**
Numbers 10–36	Israel's journey towards Canaan (some laws)
Deuteronomy	laws given beyond the Jordan (some narrative)
Joshua	Israel's occupation of Canaan: God's promise fulfilled

The first is the exodus – the time of Moses, in fact. The story of creation introduces the story of redemption. The God who redeemed Israel is identified as the creator of the world. Now the opening chapters of Genesis describe how the created world went wrong: they look forward to the story of redemption and describe how God did not just abandon his world. As its creator he cares enough about the world to redeem it.

But the link between the creation and the exodus is made via the story of Israel's ancestors – Abraham, Isaac, Jacob, Joseph, and so on. The significance of these stories, which tell the immediate pre-history of Israel, is that they record the promises of God which the act of God in the exodus fulfilled. They show that the exodus was not a casual act without forethought. God had committed himself to be Abraham's God, to make his family a nation, to give it a land – and he is fulfilling those promises.

The second situation with which we can connect Genesis is the peak of Israel's history which was constituted by the achievements of David and Solomon. Now Israel has a new position in the world – she is a mighty nation, with other peoples beneath her. The creation story reminds her of the temptations of power, of the lure of the serpent (an important symbol in Canaanite religion), of what was God's purpose for the world of which Israel is lord. The story of Abraham reminds her of the promise of God which has now received even fuller fulfilment, of the links between Israel's ancestors and the city of Jerusalem – there Melchizedek honoured Abraham (Genesis 14), there Abraham was willing to sacrifice Isaac (Genesis 22). The story of Joseph reminds her of how God works in unseen ways, through men's decisions, and how he somehow makes all things work together for good for his people – as he did in the events that brought Solomon to the throne.

The third situation with which we can connect Genesis is the exile. In this time of disaster Genesis brings a similar message to that of the prophets of that time such as Ezekiel (see p. 102). It asserts that God is a God of grace and thus suggests that all is not lost when we fail: God can still be faithful. It emphasizes the unearned goodness of God in the initial creation. It asserts the continuing faithfulness of God at the time of the flood – disaster may come but it is not God's last word. It reminds Israel that God's promises to Abraham were given before Abraham did anything to earn God's favour. It is this same point in Genesis which Paul appeals to much later (Romans 4). All Abraham did was believe God's promise – he was treated as God's man on the strength of just that. Now, in the exile, the story suggests, you are challenged to believe God's promise again.

The point is made in Genesis by describing the covenants God made with Noah (chapter 9) and Abraham (chapter 15). God's covenant relationship with his people did not begin at the exodus (when the law was given) but much earlier (before there was any law to obey). This relationship is one of grace – it stems simply from God's goodness.

The relationship between Genesis and the exile appears in the particular Jewish practices which the stories mention. In exile the distinctive outward marks of a Jew have always been important: a Jew is one who observes the sabbath, one who keeps the basic kosher law (avoiding consuming blood by draining it from an animal when it is killed), one who is circumcised. In exile the challenge to a Jew is to be willing to stand out by such practices.

Now Genesis helps him to meet this challenge, by asserting that these practices have an authority even greater than the Mosaic law. Circumcision goes back to Abraham (chapter 17). The kosher law goes back to Noah (9.4). And the Sabbath goes back to the pattern of God's own activity at creation: he did his week's work and then rested (2.2). The importance of these marks of a Jew is thus heavily underlined.

It is worth emphasizing how these stories relate to periods in Israel's life because this helps to short-circuit the problems that arise when they are treated as scientific narratives. There are indeed various ways of fitting scientific discoveries and the creation stories together. But we miss the point of Genesis if we concentrate on this question. Genesis is concerned to bring a message to people in its day that will help them to understand their own lives and help them to follow the truth. Its question is not, was the world created in six days or not? – but rather, was the world created in a purposeful way at all? Or was it rather the result of bickering among the gods, as the Babylonians thought? Or was it just an accident, as modern scientists have to believe if they are not Christians? Genesis asserts that the world was planned by someone and belongs to someone.

THE PROMISE TO ISRAEL'S ANCESTORS (Genesis 12–50)
So the story of the world leads into the story of one family. Abraham's clan are called from Mesopotamia to Canaan. The key passage that sets the scene for the whole is God's summons to Abraham, 'Leave your native land, your relatives, and your father's home, and go to a country that I am going to show you. I will give you many descendants, and they will become a great nation. I will bless you and make your name famous, so that you will be a blessing. I will bless those who bless you, but I will curse those who curse you. And through you I will bless all the nations.'(12.1–3)

The promise is restated several times in Genesis, and the stories of Abraham, Isaac, Jacob, and Joseph illustrate how it is fulfilled in part in their lifetimes. These stories also show how the promise is often in danger of *not* being fulfilled: the ancestors are not plastic heroes but real men who make man-size mistakes and ever threaten to lose what they hope to gain.

It is worth looking at these chapters against three backgrounds, as we have suggested above. First, the promise of a land leads directly to the story of the Israelites' exodus from Egypt. The promise that inspired Moses was that 'the God of the ancestors' was now fulfilling his undertaking to give his people a permanent home in Canaan (Exodus 3). And when the Israelites had escaped from Egypt, it was in the conviction that God had already promised to give them the land that, under Joshua, they invaded it (Joshua 1). At the end of their campaigns Joshua was able to testify that 'the Lord your God has given you all the good things that he promised. Every promise he made has been kept; not one has failed'. (Joshua 23.14)

THE FAMILY OF ABRAHAM

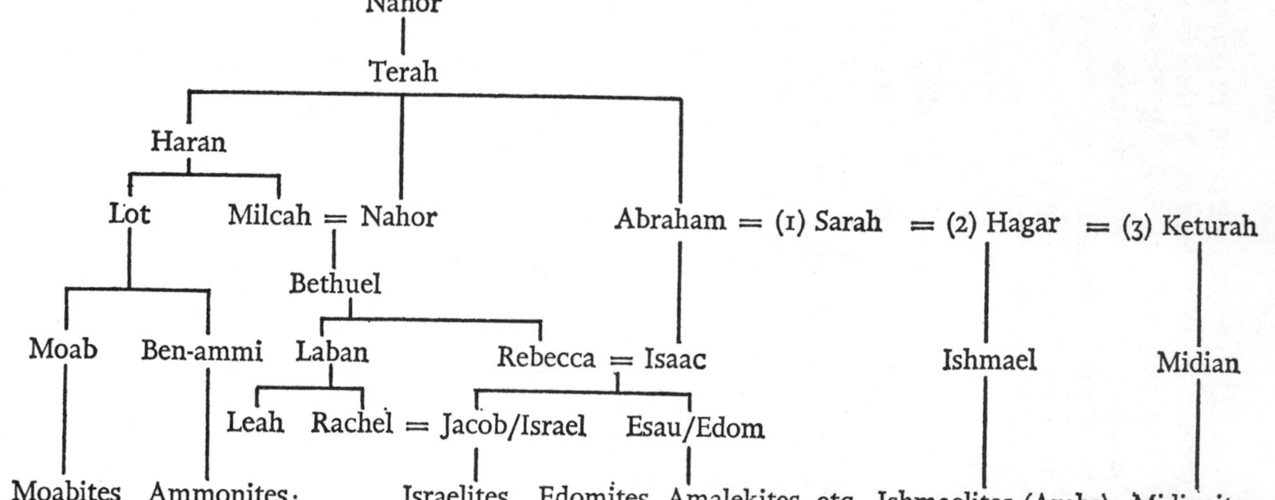

The Sons of Jacob (the heads of the Israelite tribes)
By Leah – Reuben, Simeon, Levi, Judah, Issachar, Zebulun
By Rachel's maid, Bilhah – Dan, Naphtali
By Leah's maid, Zilpah – Gad, Asher
By Rachel – Joseph, Benjamin

In this genealogy, children are not necessarily listed in order of age (e.g. Jacob was younger than Esau).

Secondly, these stories spoke powerfully in the time of David and Solomon. They refer to Judah (David and Solomon's tribe) ruling Israel (Genesis 49.10). They declare Israel's right to possess the land of Canaan – the Canaanites were cast out by God because of their wickedness (15.16). But Israel must avoid falling into Canaanite ways, even though (indeed especially if) they take over Melchizedek's city Jerusalem and identify their God Yahweh with his God El Elyon, the God Most High (14.22). They are called to be especially Yahweh's people, and to show the world what Yahweh's blessing is (12.1–3). For as Genesis 1–11 is the story of man's falling under God's curse, now God is beginning to bring man under the blessing, and he is doing that by showing what he can do with one family. He will attract others to himself by how he blesses this one. Israel's specialness is to be that she fulfils this role. The stories are an invitation and a challenge.

In the exile, the stories have a new message. Israel is once again cut off from the promised land. But the promises still stand. Israel had started off as a people with nothing, but that had not stopped God giving and fulfilling his promises to them. He could do so again, and the Israelites could take courage. All they had to do was to accept their calling: to the sabbath and the kosher law the story of Abraham adds the covenant-sign of circumcision, the sign for a Jew that he was willing to be marked out as God's man.

The fact that these stories were especially meaningful in different periods reminds us of a point we noted at the beginning of this chapter. We are not here reading mere history – mere incidents from the life of nomads of antiquity. We are reading stories that were preserved over centuries because they said something about God and man, or more specifically about God and Israel. They are sometimes called 'saga', and this is a helpful word. They are not mere fiction: they are about real people. But nor are they mere history: they are about people whose experiences later generations can identify with, and the way they are written reflects that conviction. They are stories in which every generation can see itself.

FROM EGYPT TO THE PROMISED LAND

The theme of promise and fulfilment is one that runs through the opening books of the Bible. God promises to Abraham's family that he will make them a great nation, that he will make his own covenant with them, and that he will give them a land of their own (Genesis 17). This promise is reasserted several times in Genesis, but the book sees little evidence of its fulfilment. Abraham's family grows, but still numbers less than one hundred. They wander about in the land of Canaan, but have to leave it again. They hear God speak and worship him, yet seem to live no closer to him and to make no less of a mess of their life than do families without God. The New Testament writers were to believe that 'the promise to Abraham' was only really fulfilled through Christ; it is to him that the Old Testament promise looks forward. But within the Old Testament, the promise to Abraham begins to be fulfilled when the Israelites escape from Egypt.

The books of Exodus, Leviticus and Numbers take Israel from bondage in Egypt to meeting Yahweh at Mount Sinai, and then on to the edge of the 'promised land'. They are one continuous story, not three separate books – it is possible to subdivide them, but (as the plan on p. 38 shows) the natural breaks do not come at the end of Exodus and the end of Leviticus.

THE EXODUS STORY (Exodus 1–15)

Exodus 1–15 begins with the first stage in God's promise already fulfilled: the family have become a people. But the rest of the promise seems a long way away. They are enslaved and demoralized. It is not surprising that oppressed peoples today, such as blacks and third world nations generally, have been able to identify with Israel in Egypt. The story of their oppression has a very modern ring.

What brings them out of Egypt is something very unmodern, however. It is the hand of God. He declares he is going to fulfil his promise and thus reveal himself in a new way, as Yahweh (Jehovah) – which means something like 'the God who makes his presence felt'.

He gives this undertaking to an Israelite named Moses, who had narrowly escaped death as a child and had then been brought up in the Egyptian court. Moses now clearly takes the Israelites' side and challenges the King of Egypt to release the Israelites to go and hold a religious festival in Yahweh's honour. Moses is the means of various chastisements that seek to persuade the king to let the Israelites go, but the Egyptians continue to resist until their eldest sons are killed, and their army is destroyed at the Red Sea. (This was not what we refer to as the Red Sea but an area of marsh, probably in the region of the Suez Canal.)

The story is a dramatic and bloody one. It is typical of the way the Bible describes the real world, a world very like that which we see portrayed on the television news today. Exodus declares that Yahweh involved himself in this world and in fact proved that he was God and that the king and the gods of Egypt were not. He could beat them at their own game.

The triumph of the exodus became a central feature in the Jews' thinking. It had proved that God was with them. It was the basis of the demands he made on their lives. And it suggested the way they hoped he would act in their lives in the future, when they would experience a 'new exodus' (especially at the time of the renewed bondage of the exile).

It was even supposed to be the basis of a change in the way they reckoned time: they were to make the festival of Passover (when God 'passed over' the Israelites at the time of his judgement on the Egyptians, chapter 12) the beginning of their year from now on. Probably it was especially at the Passover Festival that they told the exodus story – and thus preserved and developed the story we now have in Exodus 1–15.

One of the important features of the Israelites' faith was their belief that their God was working out a purpose in their history. Of course other nations assumed that their gods were involved in their national fortunes. If things went wrong, the gods must be displeased for some reason. (People tend to make the same assumption today!)

Israel's assumptions about God and history were more deeply thought out. Her story was not a chapter of accidents, but one in which God was involved from start to finish, in the big events and the everyday routine. He was not just the one who started the world going, or even just the power behind nature, nor was he only interested in people's religious observances. He was the God behind the events in the newspapers. Although his purpose in all those events cannot necessarily be seen straight away (unless there is a prophet to tell us what they mean), there *is* a purpose at work in them.

This basic conviction of Israel's goes back to the exodus, when Yahweh first involved himself in a nation's history and rescued an oppressed people from her affliction.

ISRAEL AT MOUNT SINAI (Exodus 16–Numbers 10)
After the excitement of the exodus story, the account of Israel's two-month stay near Mount Sinai seems tedious, and readers of the Bible often get stuck here. At a first reading, it is worth simply following the basic story-outline of the making, breaking, and remaking of the 'covenant' (the first column on the diagram which follows on p. 49). The bulk of the rest of the chapters (the second column) are concerned with the setting up of Israel's fundamental religious institutions – the sacred tent, the priesthood, and the holy camp. The remainder is made up of collections of laws that relate to Israel's religious life. Most of this material we shall deal with in chapter 9 below, on Israel's laws.

What is worth noting here, however, is that the laws in the Bible do not appear on their own but only in the context of the story. As we have already noted, *torah* embraces both story and law.

In many ways the content of the Old Testament laws is similar to those of other ancient near eastern peoples. But these laws appear in a distinctive context in the Old Testament because they are linked with the story of what Yahweh did for Israel. There are several ways of understanding this link, and all may be appropriate at different points. The ten commandments (Exodus 20) begin, 'I am the Lord your God who brought you out of Egypt, where you were slaves. Worship no god but me. Do not make for yourselves images . . .' God seems

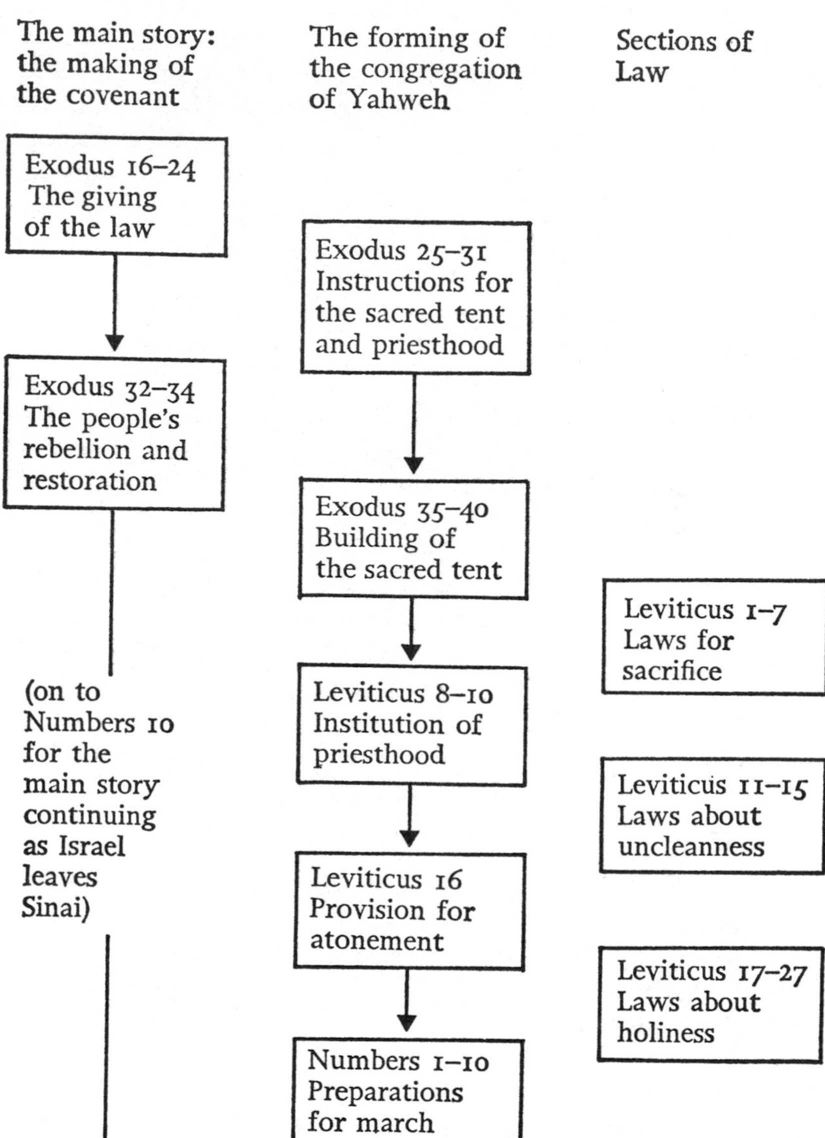
The main story: the making of the covenant
The forming of the congregation of Yahweh
Sections of Law
Exodus 16–24 The giving of the law
Exodus 25–31 Instructions for the sacred tent and priesthood
Exodus 32–34 The people's rebellion and restoration
Exodus 35–40 Building of the sacred tent
Leviticus 1–7 Laws for sacrifice
(on to Numbers 10 for the main story continuing as Israel leaves Sinai)
Leviticus 8–10 Institution of priesthood
Leviticus 11–15 Laws about uncleanness
Leviticus 16 Provision for atonement
Leviticus 17–27 Laws about holiness
Numbers 1–10 Preparations for march

to imply that his act of rescuing Israel gives him the right to declare how she should live. He has shown himself to be the God of justice; therefore she is to be just. He has shown himself to be holy; therefore she is to be holy. Such an approach might make the law sound a burden (as it appeared in New Testament times). But two other ways of linking faith and law qualify this. One is that Israel in fact saw God's law as his gracious gift to Israel. It was not a collection of limitations imposed by God, but a body of loving guidance to lead God's people in the best way. Bringing Israel out of Egypt and giving her his law are both the outworking of his grace. The other way is to see the obeying of God's laws as the grateful and appropriate response which God's people give to what he has done on his people's behalf. We shall examine this insight when we look at Deuteronomy.

A surprising feature at the heart of this story is the account of the breaking and remaking of the covenant. Hardly had Moses disappeared up Mount Sinai when Israel indulged in the idolatry that was forbidden by the commandments – not the worship of a different god, but the representation of Yahweh by means of something man created (Exodus 32). Yahweh stopped short of destroying the whole people for this, but the story makes clear that the sin of the Garden of Eden (where man immediately broke the one law God gave him) is going to characterize the story of the people of God too. Israel is only a nation of human beings.

THE JOURNEY TO THE EDGE OF THE PROMISED LAND (Numbers 11–36)

The motif of rebellion which we meet in the Sinai story runs through this next section. Even before the Israelites reached Sinai they had doubted the goodwill and the power of Moses and Yahweh (Exodus 15–17). This note dominates the book of Numbers. In effect it constitutes a turning back on the purpose for which Yahweh had called Israel. The people wish they had never left Egypt. Yahweh in fact declares that, because of their unfaith, the whole generation will not be allowed to enter the promised land (Numbers 14), and so for a generation the people live a nomadic life in the northern part of the Sinai peninsula and the Negev. There was nothing inherently dangerous or strange about this: other peoples lived nomadic lives in this area, then as now. But it was a chastisement for Israel in that it meant a delay in the fulfilment of God's promise to give them a land.

As Israel reached the edge of the promised land, they met up with 'Balaam the son of Beor' (Numbers 22–24). Here the theme of blessing and cursing, which appears in Genesis in connection with the giving of God's promise, reappears near the end of Genesis-Numbers as the fulfilment of the promise draws near. Balaam was hired to curse Israel, and thus bring trouble upon them. But he finds he is only able to bless them – to promise that they will enjoy power and prosperity. As God had once said to Abraham, Balaam declares 'whoever blesses Israel will be blessed' (Numbers 24.9). As we have noted in connection with Genesis, such a story will have spoken powerfully not only to the exodus generation, but also to those who lived (for instance) in the time of Solomon, when the promise of blessing was most clearly fulfilled, and in the exile, when Israel lived again only on the edge of the promised land and in need of God's promise of blessing to be fulfilled once more.

5

From triumph to defeat:

Deuteronomy to Kings

We noted at the beginning of the last chapter that, although Deuteronomy belongs to the *Torah* as one of the 'books of Moses', it also looks forward to Joshua, Samuel and Kings. Deuteronomy gives Israel the basis for her life in Canaan; the books which follow describe how she conquered the land, but how in the end she failed to cope with the problems she met there, because she failed to take the Deuteronomic law seriously.

The final version which we have of the books from Deuteronomy to Kings belongs, then, to the exile – which is where the story leaves off in 2 Kings. But of course these books include much material which belongs to earlier centuries, from the twelfth to the sixth century. As with the books from Genesis to Numbers, then, these subsequent books can be read at several levels – they can tell us both about the times to which they refer, and about the faith of the period in which they were actually written.

DEUTERONOMY

Deuteronomy is Moses' last speech before his death just the other side of the Jordan. It is really more of a sermon than a speech, and is full of exhortations to take God seriously. Moses keeps urging, 'Hear, O Israel, the statutes and ordinances which I speak in your hearing this day, and you shall learn them, and be careful to do them'; 'Love the Lord your God, and keep his commandments always.'

More clearly than any other part of the Bible, Deuteronomy pictures the relationship between God and his people in the light of the relationship between a great king and his underlings. We know something of this relationship from the political treaties of the day. In these, the great king reminds his subject peoples of how relationships between them have been in the past; he describes the attitude of loyalty he expects in the future, and may make specific requirements about the conducting of their affairs; and he reminds them of the consequences, good and bad, which will follow from loyalty or disloyalty.

Moses' sermon in Deuteronomy follows this pattern:

1–3 reminder of the past relationship

4–11 the attitude God requires now

12–26 the specific requirements of God

These laws are much longer than one would expect in a document based on a treaty.

Deuteronomy is influenced by eastern law-codes as well as by eastern treaties.

27–28 the consequences that will follow

29–33 closing words

These include some further features reminiscent of the treaties, such as the writing down of the document and its placing in the temple.

We will look at the laws in chapter 9. But it is worth noting here that the first of them, which required Israel to worship only in the place that the Lord chose, was of key significance in the reform of Judah's last good king, Josiah. This reform included the implementation of what was required by a lawbook found in the temple store in Jerusalem (2 Kings 22), and this lawbook was apparently what we call Deuteronomy. The influence of the Deuteronomic approach to things can be seen also in the book of Jeremiah (who also lived in this period) and in the books of Kings themselves (which were completed soon after). The distinctive phrases and emphases of Deuteronomy also appear here.

The importance of worshipping only where the Lord chose lay in the concern shared by all these books for loyalty to the

God of Israel. There were places of worship all over Canaan, and it was natural for Israelites who lived in different parts of the land to worship at these. But the origin of these shrines lay in the religion of the Canaanites, with its concern with fertility and its worship of Baal. It was difficult for the Israelites to avoid being influenced by this religion, and Deuteronomy seeks to guard against it. Loyalty to the Lord is of fundamental significance. Josiah took 'the place that the Lord chooses' to be Jerusalem, though Deuteronomy itself (with its setting beyond the Jordan) does not say this.

JOSHUA

The book of Joshua is the story of Joshua. It begins with his challenge to Israel at the beginning of her period of leadership, as Israel still waits encamped the other side of the Jordan. It ends with his challenge to Israel at the end of his life, as Israel begins her settled life west of the Jordan. In between these two gatherings, the first half of the book describes how Joshua led Israel in her conquest of the land, the second half tells how he distributed the land among the Israelite tribes.

1 initial challenge
2–12 conquest of the land
13–22 distribution of the land
23–24 closing challenge

Following the pentateuch, the book of Joshua tells how the plan of God was finally accomplished. The undertaking which God had made back in Abraham's day is fulfilled; the purpose he initiated through Moses is completed. 'Not one thing has failed of all the good things which the Lord your God promised concerning you' (23.14).

As we find with some other books, however, within this united structure of the book of Joshua, very diverse material is included. There are the speeches, which express the teaching of Deuteronomy and challenge Israel to obey God both as she conquers the land and in her life there. There are the exciting tales of the spies and Rahab (chapter 2), the capture of Jericho (chapter 6), the sin of Achan at Ai (chapter 7–8), the cleverness of the Gibeonites (chapter 9), the slaughter of the kings on the day the sun stood still (chapter 10). There are the more terse notes of the military statistics of Joshua's campaigns. There are the detailed records regarding which village was to belong to whom. The variety of material in this book opens the door on the variety of the life of Israel, the many different contexts in which the material that eventually made up the Bible was preserved (the sanctuary, the camp-fire, the records office), and the variety of significance which the material must have had for the Israelites (exhortation, entertainment, historical interest, legal need).

The book was actually composed in the exile, however, and in this context its message is clear. Israel is once again outside her promised land, but the book of Joshua reminds her that the land was won at the first by the Lord's gift – so he could do it again. The land had been distributed among the tribes at the Lord's bidding – it belonged to him, and he could give it to them again. The challenge to them was to respond to Joshua's challenge to take the laws of God seriously.

Stressing that the land was given by God, the major part of the book emphasizes one side of the story of how Israel came to possess the land. It is aware, however, that there were other aspects to the story than the glorious conquest. The final chapter, with its challenge to an apparently mixed audience to make up their minds to serve Yahweh, hints that many of the later 'Israelites' had lived in the land before the conquest, and now joined the invaders who were perhaps their relatives. The opening chapter of the next book adds another dimension to the picture of the process whereby the land came to belong to Israel.

JUDGES TO I SAMUEL 7

The excitement of the book of Joshua is followed by a telling footnote, which is now the introduction to the book of Judges. We might well have inferred from Joshua that the conquest was gloriously consummated. But now we learn that there were certain areas not conquered – the most difficult ones, in fact, areas where the more sophisticated Canaanites were concentrated. There thus remains a challenge before Israel; to enter fully into the inheritance God has given them, to mop up the not insignificant remains of the Canaanites.

In fact, the story has to relate a series of disasters, all following the same pattern. This pattern is announced by chapters 2–3.

1) The Israelites become unfaithful to their God.
2) The Lord is angry with them and allows them to be oppressed by enemies.
3) In response to their pleas for help the Lord raises up a 'judge' or deliverer to defeat their enemies.
4) The land has rest until the Israelites fall into sin again.

The stories that follow introduce us to some of the most exciting Old Testament figures: Deborah (chapters 4–5), Gideon (6–8), Samson (13–16), and others of whom much less is told. The stories recount events that happened to different clans in different parts of the land over a period of two centuries from Joshua to Saul. The book as a whole casts them into the framework of the pattern described above, seeing them all as events in the life of the whole people of God.

The scene is increasingly one of moral, religious and political anarchy, and the later chapters make it clear that they understood the problem to be the fact that 'everyone did just as he pleased' because 'there was no king in Israel at that time' (Judges 21.25). The book thus prepares the way for the institution of the monarchy in 1 Samuel. The first chapters of 1 Samuel essentially belong to the judges sequence, for the oppression of the Philistines, which leads to Saul's taking office, is the last and most awful example of the cycle of sin and tragedy that runs through Judges.

We may again see the composition of this book as a whole as designed to speak to the people in exile. Here they have fallen into the deepest sin (1) and experienced the deepest affliction (2). But perhaps the pattern can be completed again: if they turn back to the Lord he may restore them (3) and they may once again enjoy rest in the land (4).

The story from Joshua to 2 Kings is a continuous one, and any subdivisions, whether those made in the present form of the biblical text itself, or the alternatives we suggest here, need to be seen as marking the 'chapters' of a longer whole.

As we have seen, the beginning of 1 Samuel describes the final and greatest of the crises of the period of the judges. Again the people sin, again the Lord punishes, again they pray, again the Lord restores: and now the new 'chapter' begins, for the one through whom the answer comes is not merely a judge, but a king.

Kings will be a mixed blessing, and the ambiguity of the institution of the monarchy is reflected in the story of its origin. The story so far has prepared us to see kings as a good thing, because the alternative is the ever deeper chaos of the period of the judges. And yet God is supposed to be Israel's king, so her request for a human monarch is a rejection of him. This attitude appears also in the earlier chapters of Judges: Gideon, for instance, refuses to be made king (8.23).

Only three kings ruled over the united nation. Each begins as a hero but ends as a tragedy. Saul wins some splendid victories but is immediately involved in the tension that is to bedevil many kings, that between exercising powerful leadership and doing what the situation demands, on the one hand, and obeying God, especially in the form of his word through his prophets, on the other. Because he gives priority to the former, Saul is rejected, and he soon begins to show symptoms of psychosis in his attitude to his general David, whose achievements and popularity are threatening to eclipse his king's. Saul finally dies, a lonely and tragic figure, totally defeated by his enemies, and alienated from his God as well as from former associates such as Samuel and David.

David has already taken over the status of the hero of the story before he actually comes to the throne. Probably the story goes back to David's reign, so it is not surprising that he is the hero! Nevertheless a remarkable feature of the portrait of David is its ambiguity. Is he the man with an eye for the main chance, the man who falls on his feet? Or the man who seeks to go God's way, the man whom God consequently blesses? The story can be read both ways. What is indisputable is the military achievement of David in disposing of the Philistine threat once and for all, and in building the biggest empire Israel ever knew.

The tragedy of David, as the later chapters of 2 Samuel show, was that his gifts as a general were not matched by a wisdom in personal relationships. These chapters (which probably go back to Solomon's reign) reveal a story of sin and incompetence which is only too human. And yet, the story implies, God's providence is able to achieve what he wanted through it all: Solomon becomes king.

Solomon's story, too, begins with his achievement: supremely, the building of a temple for Yahweh, though also other buildings in Jerusalem and elsewhere, and the consolidation and organization of the empire inherited from David. The tragedy of Solomon was that 'he loved many foreign women' (1 Kings 11): the sin is not the polygamy but the opening of the door to the influence of alien religions in Israel. Kings sees this as the key to the downfall of Israel's state in the short and the long term.

1 KINGS 12—2 KINGS 25

After Solomon, the books of Kings tell the complicated, interwoven story of the two kingdoms of (northern) Israel and Judah until the national existence of both came to an end. The major question posed by the books from Joshua to Kings – why did Israel and Judah fall? – is now in the forefront of the presentation. The answer is that, by and large, the kings of Israel and Judah failed to lead their peoples in the ways of David, who for all his personal faults is regarded as a paradigm of faithfulness to Yahweh. On the contrary, they repeatedly encouraged Israel and Judah to follow the Baals, the local gods of the Canaanites, who were worshipped at shrines all over the country.

The pattern of the books is to introduce each king with his date, his family background, and a general judgement on his reign along the lines just described, then sometimes to relate particular events from his reign, then to tell of his death and who succeeded him. 2 Kings 12, the story of Joash, provides a straightforward example of the pattern.

Several of the kings are regarded as particularly significant. Northern Israel's first king, Jeroboam, is the archetypal villain. He first set his country on the wrong road by taking her away from the worship of Yahweh in Jerusalem (1 Kings 12–13), and it is because they followed his way that the Israelites were cast off (2 Kings 17). Judah's equivalent to Jeroboam is Manasseh (2 Kings 21). He is Judah's archetypal villain, and is blamed for the final fall of Judah (2 Kings 24).

Either side of Manasseh are described the only two kings who are assessed very positively, Hezekiah (2 Kings 18–20), and Josiah (2 Kings 22–23). These uniquely 'did what was pleasing to the Lord' and walked in the ways of David; but they were not able to avert the fate towards which kings such as Manasseh were hurrying the nation.

As well as emphasizing the responsibility of the kings as those who led their people in the right or the wrong way, and the importance of loyalty to Jerusalem, its temple, and its worship as a criterion of true religion, Kings stresses the role of the prophets of Yahweh in the story of the two kingdoms. Kings gives many chapters to the stories of Elijah and Elisha, and at other key points introduces a prophet who brings God's word to a situation and thus is either the means of God blessing his people or, more often, of bringing a warning of judgement.

Overall, the books of Kings tell a gloomy story. And yet in the exile they offer a few glimmers of hope. The reforms of Hezekiah and Josiah had not been ignored by God – God honours those who turn to him. It might still be so. God had committed himself to the line of David: he might still concern himself with David's people. Indeed the last paragraph of the books tells of the release of the heir to David's throne, who had been imprisoned in Babylon: and it hints that, despite the gloominess of the story, God may not yet have finished with Israel.

6

The story of the community:

Chronicles, Ezra, Nehemiah

With 1 Chronicles we find ourselves back precisely where we started, with Adam. 1 and 2 Chronicles in fact retell the story from Genesis to Kings.

They tell the story from a different perspective, however. In some ways it is only a sharpened version of the perspective of Kings, for one important theme of Kings was Jerusalem and the temple, and these are even more central in Chronicles. In fact, nearly everything that does not directly deal with Jerusalem and the temple is omitted.

Thus the whole history up to Saul is compressed into eight introductory chapters of genealogies. The real story begins with David, who planned the temple, and Solomon, who built it. In their reigns, anything that merely concerned their private lives or their secular activities is omitted as irrelevant. But what concerns the temple and its worship is retained and expanded. After them, the history of northern Israel is quietly and totally omitted: when the northern tribes cut themselves off from Jerusalem, they cut themselves off from the story of God's people. Even the great stories of Elijah and Elisha disappear because of the authors' desire to concentrate on this chosen theme.

A comparison of Chronicles and Samuel–Kings shows that it not only covers the same ground. The author actually copied much of his material from the earlier work. Whole sections in Chronicles follow the text of Samuel–Kings, as can be seen by comparing the chapters referred to in the GNB section headings. Some of these sections have additions made to them. Other whole sections, as we have already noted, are quite omitted: they are irrelevant to the message the author wants to bring.

THE STORY OF THE COMMUNITY: CHRONICLES, EZRA, NEHEMIAH

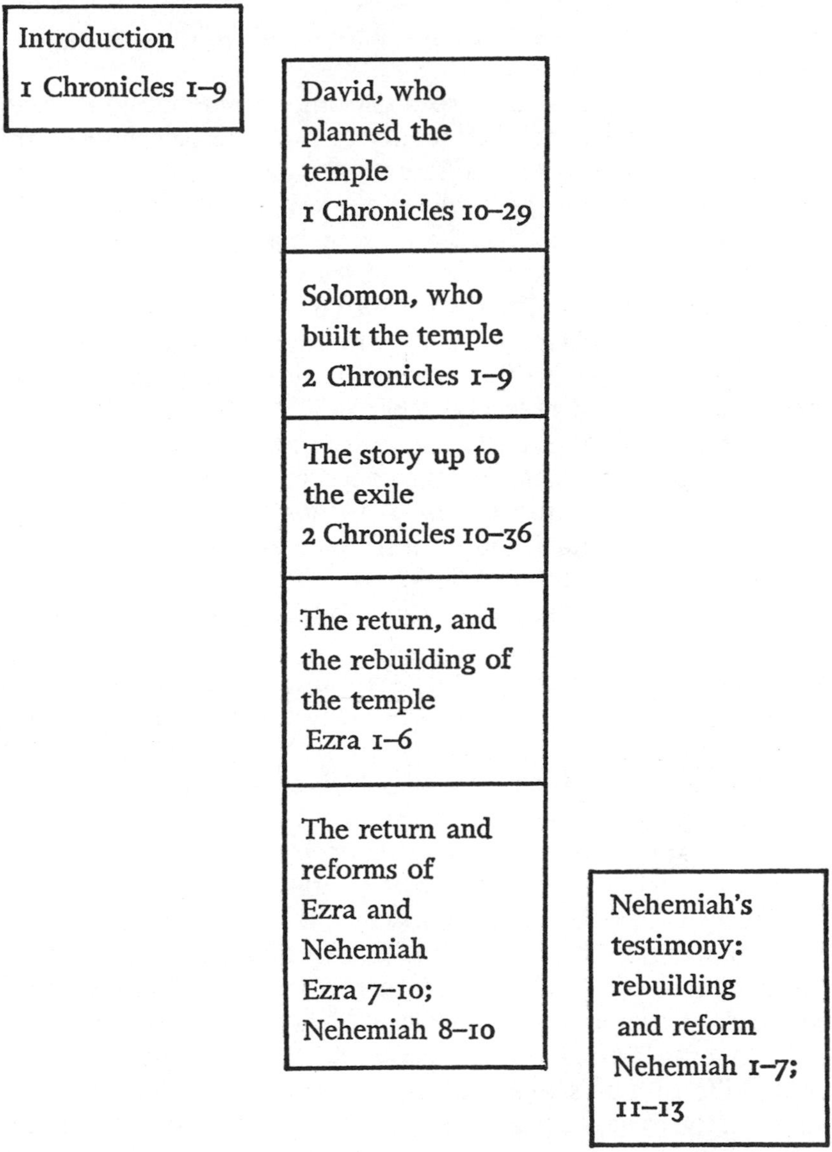

Introduction
1 Chronicles 1–9

David, who planned the temple
1 Chronicles 10–29

Solomon, who built the temple
2 Chronicles 1–9

The story up to the exile
2 Chronicles 10–36

The return, and the rebuilding of the temple
Ezra 1–6

The return and reforms of Ezra and Nehemiah
Ezra 7–10; Nehemiah 8–10

Nehemiah's testimony: rebuilding and reform
Nehemiah 1–7; 11–13

They are in effect replaced by extra material on the life of David, Hezekiah, Josiah, etc. Many of these extra stories are dramatic accounts of famous victories in war, won against great odds.

Often the only sections from Chronicles which people read (for instance, in Church Lectionary or Bible Study schemes) are the ones which supplement Samuel–Kings – and then only the interesting ones! But the books as a whole deserve to be read in their own right. They have a clear message which relates to the very different period in which they were written.

We have seen that Kings was written in the exile. It admitted Israel's sin and perhaps hinted at the hope that she might one day be restored again. But when this restoration came a few years later, she did not regain her political freedom. She was now a religious community under foreign overlords, rather as Jews were in Europe earlier this century. So the temple and its worship were even more central to her faith than they had been before the exile, and Chronicles was written to tell the story of the temple for people for whom it was all-important.

The story is continued in Ezra, which describes how the temple was rebuilt and its worship reconstituted. The books of Ezra and Nehemiah are a continuation of the books of Chronicles. Having described the restoration of the temple, they tell how the life of the community in Jerusalem was reordered under the leadership of Ezra and Nehemiah, emissaries from the Persian court.

There are no kings descended from David whose story can be told now, of course: there were no kings after the exile. The compiler of Chronicles is interested in David not because there were Davidic kings in his day, nor (probably) because he is looking forward to a day when there will once again be a king on David's throne; but because it was David who laid the plans and made the provisions for the temple, which is now the heart of the life of God's people. God has fulfilled the promises he made in the exile, not indeed by giving his people political independence again, but by returning to the temple which he had left because of his peoples's sin.

So Chronicles goes into detail in connection with the temple, dwelling on its planning by David (1 Chronicles 21–29), its building by Solomon (2 Chronicles 2–7) and the various reforms of its worship (Hezekiah, 2 Chronicles 29–31; Josiah, 2 Chronicles 34–35). Ezra's account of the restoration of the Jews from exile centres on the rebuilding of the temple. Cyrus commanded the Jews to return for this purpose (Ezra 1), the first act of those Jews who returned was to recommence worship in the broken-down building and to initiate rebuilding (Ezra 3), and the story of the return comes to a triumphant and joyful climax with the completion of this project (Ezra 5–6). For the temple is the very life centre of the people.

Chronicles naturally concerns itself with the worship of the temple, and often notes in detail how the ritual laws were kept. It describes the various ministries exercised in the temple. Naturally the priests, with their important responsibility in offering sacrifice, are prominent. But more striking is the frequent mention of the Levites (the priests' assistants, according to Deuteronomy) – some scholars have inferred the writer must have been a Levite himself! They are the leaders of worship and singing in the temple; Chronicles emphasizes the joyful praise of Israel's worship, which is the very heart of what it means to be the people of God. Striking, too, is the frequent appearance of prophets in the Chronicler's picture of the temple worship. If they are critical of Israel's worship, it is from within the institution, rather than from outside it: they urge the congregation to order their worship aright.

As we have noted, northern Israel loses its place in the history of the people of God, because it cut itself off from David, from Jerusalem, and from the temple. Nevertheless, the door remains open to Israel to return: and the door is also open to foreigners to be involved in the service of God. Even so, the overall emphasis of Chronicles–Ezra–Nehemiah is to be wary of alien influence. One feature of the life of the times was evidently the danger that the Jews would lose their identity and become indistinguishable from other peoples in the area. The books of Ezra and Nehemiah speak of other people who wanted to join in the rebuilding of the temple, and of mixed marriages between Jews and Ammonites, Moabites, etc. The books take a hard line on these issues, out of their concern that the people of God should not lose their purity and their distinctiveness.

So God's people, as Chronicles–Ezra–Nehemiah sees them, are in a privileged, but an insecure position. The thrust is thus to emphasize that they are called to trust and obey God. The books, in story and sermon, keep reminding them of the characteristics of God which ought to stimulate them to this life of faith. He is the mighty God who makes it possible for his people to win battles against impossible odds, the just God who honours those who honour him but sees that the wicked get their deserts, the faithful God who fulfils his word, the gracious God who forgives and restores those who return to him. So people can afford to trust him, and cannot afford not to obey him, in their everyday lives.

7

Short Stories:

Ruth, Esther, Jonah and Daniel

Within the books we have already considered are included sections that probably once existed on their own. Among these are the stories of Joseph (in Genesis), of how Solomon came to succeed to the throne (in Samuel–Kings), of Nehemiah (in the book of Nehemiah). Other stories were not incorporated into the great history works, but stand on their own.

RUTH

The book of Ruth is the tale of a Moabite girl who married into an Israelite family which was staying in Moab (east of the Jordan) during a famine. After the tragic death of her husband and her father-in-law, Ruth accompanies her mother-in-law, Naomi, back to the family village, Bethlehem. There she wins the love of another man from Naomi's family, Boaz, who marries her and brings comfort to Naomi as the couple present her with a grandchild.

That is a bald summary of the plot of the story, but nevertheless it may hint at how charming a story it is in its own right, before one begins to ask why it is in the Bible. It is remarkable for its open attitude to its foreign heroine, which perhaps contrasts with the attitude taken by Ezra and Nehemiah to such peoples as the Moabites. The openness is the more remarkable when we reach what may be the punch-line of the story in the closing paragraph. It transpires that the son of Ruth and Boaz is the grandfather of the mighty King David: a worthy reward for the courage and loyalty of Ruth, and the chivalry of Boaz.

JONAH

The story of Jonah is set two or three centuries later, in the time of the northern Israelite kingdom. Jonah was an Israelite prophet (his book appears among the 'twelve prophets', see pp. 104–7), commissioned by God to go and preach in Nineveh. Not warming to this calling, he caught a ship going in the opposite direction, but found he could not so easily escape God, who sent a storm after him. To rescue the ship from God's anger, Jonah lets himself be thrown overboard; to rescue Jonah from the sea, God sends a fish to catch him and take him back to land. Having learned his lesson, Jonah proceeds to Nineveh, and to his disgust convinces the Ninevites that they should repent and avoid God's judgement. The final scene pictures Jonah's further disgust at God's permitting the death of a tree which had given him shade; God points out that his concern for the tree makes a strange contrast with his lack of concern for the Ninevites.

If the charm of Ruth is evident from the plot, the humour of Jonah will be clear from this outline. Jonah is, at point after point, an illustration of how not to be a prophet. In particular, like Ruth, the book suggests that God often has a much more positive attitude to those who do not (yet) belong to his people, than those people themselves have.

ESTHER

Our third 'short story' is a grimmer tale. The scene is the court of the Persian King, Artaxerxes. The king's prime minister, Haman, persuades him to authorize the elimination of the Jewish population of the empire, and many of the Persian peoples prepare to implement the order. It happens to be the case that one of the king's wives, Esther, is a Jewess, however, while her foster-father, Mordecai, had once rescued the king from assassination. These two are able to get the tables turned in the nick of time. Haman is hanged on the gallows he prepared for Mordecai, and the Jews slaughter those who were preparing to kill them.

The bloody story epitomizes the Jews' conviction about their own history. Often blood has been shed, usually theirs. But the story embodies the belief that somehow God is in control, working out a just purpose even through the selfish decisions of men.

DANIEL

Daniel and his friends were young men transported to Babylon at the time of the exile. Two themes recur in the stories about them. The first is that of the religious challenge brought to the young men by having to live in a foreign environment. Will they keep up their distinctive way of life? Will they worship idols? Will they pray to the emperor? It is their faithfulness in these matters that leads to their being sentenced to being burnt to death or eaten alive. But God is faithful to them, as they have been to him.

The second theme of the stories is the wisdom of the young men. Babylon was a renowned intellectual centre, but it turns out that Daniel and his friends can outdo the great minds of Babylon, because of the insight their God gives them. In particular, Daniel can interpret the meaning of the king's horrendous dreams; and on top of this, he receives significant visions himself. The second half of the book concentrates on these, and we will look at them in chapter 13.

So the stories challenge the reader to be faithful to God and his law, and to trust that he is the Lord of the secrets of world history.

8

The story of Jesus and the church:

Matthew to Acts

A gospel is a unique form of writing to tell a unique kind of story. The Christian church centred its faith on a man Jesus who lived thirty-odd years. But all that was important about him (his achievements and his teaching) belong to his last three years, so they concentrate on these. And what really mattered most about him was the way his story ended: so the gospels give a third of their attention to the very last days of his life.

The four gospels are named after men we hear about in the New Testament itself. Matthew and John were among Jesus's twelve closest disciples, Mark and Luke were involved in events in the early history of the church described in the Acts of the Apostles. But the four names do not actually come in the gospels themselves, only in the headings ('According to Matthew', etc.) which were added later. So we cannot be sure whether these men were the authors of the books credited to them, though there are no more plausible candidates for the role.

The gospels were written within a few decades of the death of Christ. Most scholars date them between about 65 and 100. Luke and John tell us why they wrote, and it is not unlikely that the same concerns provided at least part of Matthew and Mark's motivation. They wrote so that people could have reliable information on the course of Jesus's ministry and on the content of his teaching, so that they could have a secure foundation for faith in him (see Luke 1.1–4; John 20.30–31).

The gospels are not biographies of Jesus. They do not describe his appearance or personality; they tell us little of his social or family background; their treatment of most of his life is very sketchy. Nor do we have any further reliable information about Jesus from outside the New Testament. Certain facts about him – that he lived, exercised a public ministry, died in the time of Pontius Pilate, and soon came to be worshipped all over the eastern Mediterranean – are referred to by the first century Jewish writer Josephus, by Jewish traditions preserved in the *Talmud*, or by Roman writers such as Pliny the Younger and Tacitus. In Christian writings outside the New Testament such as the so-called 'Gospel of Thomas', there are a few sayings which may genuinely go back to Jesus. But virtually our whole picture of his life, teaching, ministry, death, and resurrection comes from the gospels in the New Testament.

Nevertheless the basic historical accuracy of the story of Jesus was essential to the truth of the Christian message, and it was the task of the apostles to give their eye-witness testimony to what they had seen and heard of Jesus. But the apostles could not be in every place at once, and must eventually die, and one may guess that those two facts lay behind the writing of the gospels. These writings give a fixed record of the story of Jesus for those who had not known him.

Although all four gospels manifest the same general form referred to above, the first three resemble each other especially closely. They often repeat paragraphs in almost exactly the same form. These three *synoptic* gospels (the word means that they look at the story in the same way) are evidently dependent on each other. Probably Mark is the oldest of them, and his work has been used by Matthew and Luke. But Matthew and Luke also have other material in common, which does not appear in Mark, and this probably comes from another older work which has not survived on its own. This work, a collection of Jesus's teaching, is referred to as Q (from the German word *Quelle*, meaning source).

Thirty years or so separates the lifetime of Jesus from the first written gospels (though Q may have been written down in the 50s), and as far as we know, during this time the story and teaching of Jesus were passed on by word of mouth in the preaching and teaching of the church. No doubt this preaching and teaching dealt mostly with single sayings or incidents (as in our reading and preaching), and this means we cannot be sure of putting all the individual events in their chronological order. But the period involved was short, and many who had heard and seen Jesus themselves were available to provide a check on the elaboration of the story. Thus, when writers such as Mark and Luke (who refers to the fact that he was not an eye-witness himself, but made a point of gaining access to the testimony of those who were) came to produce their gospels, there was no insuperable problem involved in providing their readers with reliable information.

As we shall see, there is a very distinctive flavour about John's Gospel: we cannot even be sure he had ever seen any of the others. The history of how the gospels came into existence may thus be understood in the way that the following diagram suggests:

The life and teaching of Jesus

The preaching and teaching of the various churches:
for example

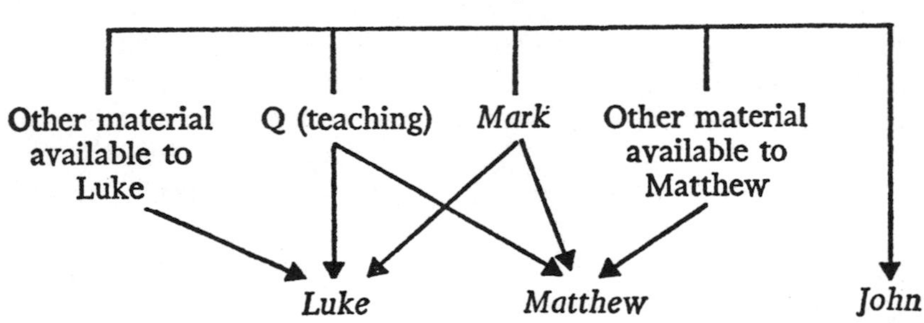

The basic theme of the gospels, particularly as the synoptics put it, is that the coming of Jesus means that God is beginning to reign on earth. Jesus declares that 'the right time has come and the Kingdom of God is near' (Mark 1.15). The title 'Kingdom of God' does not refer to a particular place, like the

'United Kingdom'. It describes 'God's ruling over the world as king' (see the GNB wordlist). The Old Testament story has shown God reigning, but only with any effectiveness over Israel, and even there only to a limited extent and for a limited time. God's reign over the world was not an observable reality. Devout Jews tried to make it a reality in their personal lives. At the same time they longed for a day when God would break into history again, vindicate his name, restore his people, punish his enemies, and fulfil his purpose. But the idea of the kingdom was in danger of dissolving into mere individual piety, or otherworldly dreaming, or only-too-worldly revolutionary politics.

Nevertheless the symbol of 'God's Kingdom' expressed some of the highest of men's aspirations and some of the basic truths concerning God's purpose, and thus Jesus took it as his basic theme and let his life (and his death) correct any misunderstanding to which the phrase was open.

As the one who was bringing God's reign, Jesus spoke with an unprecedented authority. He taught with God's authority, in fact, and invited people to learn from him the truth about God and his ways. His authority proved itself over the power of illness and demon possession and potential natural disaster – over the supernatural powers of evil, in fact, that opposed the breaking in of the reign of God. Jesus's authority won him varying degrees of allegiance from a wide variety of people – working men, agents of the Roman administration, social outcasts – though often their commitment was shallow, and Jesus made little impact on the religious leaders among the Jews.

It was the difficulty of getting right through to many of these people that led him to speak in parables. A parable is not a simple, obvious illustration of a truth that is difficult to understand. It is almost the opposite: a story that is difficult to understand which relates to a truth that is easy enough to understand but hard to accept. Whoever heard of a man paying the same wage no matter how many hours a man worked (Matthew 20.1–16); or killing the fatted calf for a renegade son while seeming to ignore his faithful brother (Luke 15.11–32)? In the parables, which show what God's reign is about, Jesus tells stories which begin in his listeners' everyday lives, but then contain a twist in the tail – and he challenges them to puzzle out how the twist in the tail illustrates the surprising ways of God.

A recurrent theme here is the rejection of those who thought they were in a privileged position, and the elevation of those who had no status at all. The reign of God is good news for those who need good news. But for those who are doing very well already, it is rather bad news, unless they can put themselves in the position of the despised outcast.

It transpires that the Jews as a whole reject Jesus. (It needs to be said that this was not because Jews are especially wicked: they were simply the religiously privileged people of the day, and if Jesus came now it would be those of us who are ministers and deacons and so on who would be most likely to be acting as the Jews did in Jesus's day.) Jesus's preaching of the Kingdom leads to his rejection and crucifixion; but that is only the beginning of another story.

Two further aspects of the story need to be mentioned here, however, though they have more systematic expression in the letters of Paul (see chapter 12).

The first is that the rejection and death of Jesus are not just an unforeseen calamity that is fortunately reversed by the resurrection. The day of Jesus's death came to be called Good Friday, and that is because his death was part of God's purpose, and was in fact not a hindrance to God ruling on earth, but a means of God ruling on earth. Here were men and devils doing their worst, but even in letting them do their worst, Jesus won a victory over them. When Jesus on the cross said, 'It is finished' (John 19.30), he meant not 'I'm done', but 'I've done it'.

That achievement – and the life he lived before his death and resurrection – raises the other question, as to who this being really was. It was a question men could hardly help asking. The popular answer of his followers was, 'He is the messiah' – the redeemer, the Davidic king the Jews had long hoped for. This was true, but misleading, because of its misleading political overtones. Jesus referred to himself in terms of the Lord's servant who accepts affliction on behalf of others (described in Isaiah 42 and 52–53), and of the 'Son of Man', the 'New Man', a triumphant but other-worldly figure. But beyond this, he manifests a uniquely close relationship with God as his Father; and John explicitly draws the inference that he is divine himself (just as I am human because my father is human). So John's gospel begins by declaring that 'the Word (the one through whom God expressed himself) became a human being' in Jesus (John 1.14), and ends by describing Thomas's acknowledgement of him as 'My Lord and my God' (John 20.28).

In many ways the story of Jesus is the story of the conflict between him and the religious parties of his day, for he was threatening the status of the established or competing with lesser groups for popular allegiance. Several groups are mentioned in the gospels.

The *Sadducees* were the official priestly families. Their name indicates that they were the descendants of the original high priestly family of Zadok (the first high priest when the temple was built by Solomon). They were very much an establishment group. Theologically, this meant they were conservative. They were deeply committed to the authority of the written law (the law of Moses), and especially emphasized the Sabbath. They did not accept the more detailed oral law which claimed to interpret what was written and to bring it up to date. Thus they were suspicious of newer doctrines such as the belief in angels and in the resurrection of the dead (see the story in Mark 12). They were also politically conservative: they were the aristocracy as well as the temple officials. They were the group closest to the political authorities (Herod and the Romans), on whom they depended for their position, and they tried to combine devotion to the law with political prudence.

The *Pharisees* were a kind of society, not a family group. Their name means 'separated ones', and has its background in the Maccabaean period (see p. 23), when the 'pious ones' (*hasidim*) supported rebellion against the Jews' Hellenistic overlords who were trying to enforce Hellenistic practices. The Pharisees accepted a thoroughgoing commitment to keeping the law, including a wide range of oral law which regulated the detailed observance of requirements such as purity, tithing, and fasting. Their concern with purity is reflected in the discussion concerning handwashing, etc., in Mark 7; and it led to a determination to avoid contact with people who did not obey the law, who were therefore impure themselves and liable to defile those who had contact with them. The Pharisees were not interested in political action, but concentrated on piety in order to prepare for the breaking in of God's kingdom. They had strong hopes of the coming of the messiah and of the resurrection of the dead. Although Jesus fulfilled these hopes, his understanding of what it meant to be the messiah was very different from theirs, and (as we have noted) he preferred to avoid that title.

The *Zealots* accepted the same theological beliefs as the Pharisees but were not satisfied with the view that the Jews simply had to wait until God brought about his kingdom. They believed they were called, like the rebels of the Maccabaean age, to refuse to submit to the Roman emperor and to take the reins of history themselves. They formed guerrilla bands in the Judaean hill country and were the driving force in the wars which led to the fall of Jerusalem in AD 70.

The *Essenes* are not mentioned in the gospels, perhaps partly as a consequence of their distinctive belief that God's people were called to separate themselves from ordinary society in an even more radical way than the Pharisees. The Essene approach is seen in its most thoroughgoing form among those Jews who left Jerusalem to form their own community in the isolation of the desert shore of the Dead Sea at Qumran. They saw the religion of the temple as corrupt, and cutting themselves off from it, sought to prepare for God's own re-establishing of true worship. Although the New Testament makes no reference to the Essenes or to Qumran, there are many parallels to their ideas and practices, such as baptism, the stress on repentance, the belief that they are the true people of God at the threshold of the messianic age, the emphasis on warfare against Satan, the picture of a conflict between flesh and spirit and between light and darkness. The difference, of course, is that the Christians believed that the messiah had come, and that his name was Jesus of Nazareth. What they had in common with the Essenes was the theological motifs used to express his significance.

The *teachers of the law*, or scribes, are the final group who need to be mentioned. They are neither a family nor a society holding particular views, but a class of men who might also be, for instance, Pharisees or Christians. They were the theologians and teachers, experts who had studied and now offered teaching to others. In their turn, they commissioned their pupils to teach within their own tradition: there were various schools and views. In a sense, Jesus may be seen as a scribe with his pupils (hence his being called *rabbi*), but there was something different about him. He taught not by reference to the teaching he had received from a master, but with his own authority (see Matthew 7.28–9).

The basic theme of the gospels, their fundamental picture of Jesus and his significance, is similar in all four accounts. But each has a distinctive slant, and needs to be considered in its own right.

MARK

We begin with what was probably the first gospel written. It is probably also the nearest to what one would have seen and heard if one had been present in Galilee or Jerusalem at the time.

Compared with the other gospels, one is struck by its brevity. It begins where Jesus's ministry begins, and has neither the kind of background that Matthew and Luke provide in their family records and accounts of Jesus's birth and boyhood, nor the elaborate theological introduction with which John prefaces his gospel. Although it includes much of the teaching of Jesus (including many of his parables), it has few of the great discourses which are prominent especially in Matthew and John. Its account of the resurrection is so succinct that it was soon felt to need supplementing by fuller accounts based on other gospels (the two 'old endings' appended in GNB).

As we read Mark in its own right, several themes strike us. The earlier part of Jesus's ministry is characterized by two contrasting features: his authoritative ministry stirs up controversy and opposition among the leaders of the Jews, but he quietly builds up a body of disciples through whom he plans to extend his work. The opposition increases, and even Jesus's family and home village reject him (6.1–4). He foresees the cross looming over the story, but his disciples cannot acknowledge it (8.31–33; 9.30–32). Opponents and disciples coalesce as Jesus is betrayed and abandoned; at his death it is a Roman centurion who recognizes that he has stood in the presence of a son of God. Suddenly we are at the end of the story: Jesus has abandoned the tomb (though the event is not described) and is off to meet his disciples again in Galilee.

MATTHEW

A clear structure can be perceived in Matthew's gospel: it is arranged so that major sections of narrative and teaching alternate.

1–2	Introduction
3–4	The beginning of Jesus's ministry
5–7	His teaching of his disciples ('the Sermon on the Mount')
8–9	Healing miracles
10	His commission of the twelve disciples
11–12	Controversies
13	His parables about the kingdom
14–17	The Path towards the cross (i)
18	His teaching on humility and forgiveness
19–22	The path towards the cross (ii)
23–25	His teaching on judgement
26–28	His death and resurrection

Matthew was a gospel written for Christians (probably especially Jews who had come to acknowledge Jesus as messiah), rather than for people who were just interested in the faith. This is apparent, for instance, in the way it systematizes Jesus's teaching on the life of discipleship (especially in the Sermon on the Mount). While Matthew will have none of the legalism of the Jews of Jesus's day, he equally has no time for Christians who do not see that their faith makes a difference to their lives.

Mere enthusiastic worship, or even miracles done in Christ's name, are not enough (7.21–7). This theme appears also in his treatment of the parables. To a greater degree than Mark he applies these to the life of the church itself. They were originally addressed, of course, to people confronted by Jesus's message in his lifetime. Now they warn Christians that they could fall into the same trap as the Jews had done, if they do not (for instance) remain faithful as they await the final coming of the kingdom. Finally, Matthew closes his gospel with the reminder that before that last day the good news of Christ has to be preached to all men, and if the church wants Christ to be with them, they will find he is with them as they fulfil this commission.

Matthew shows his concern with the relationship of Christianity to the Jewish faith in two main ways. On the one hand, he emphasizes the failure of Judaism. The lives of the Pharisees and teachers of the law – who were very upright and faithful – were not good enough. It was these so-called leaders of Judaism who rejected the Jewish messiah. On the other hand, he asserts that Christianity is the true heir to the Old Testament. He makes this point by his frequent references to the Old Testament, whose own goals he claims are fulfilled in Jesus.

LUKE AND ACTS

In broad outline, Luke, too, has a clear shape:

1–3	Introduction. Jesus's birth, his boyhood, and his baptism
4–9.50	His ministry in Galilee
9.51–19.27	His journey to Jerusalem
19.28–24.52	His final days in Jerusalem

Luke's opening paragraph (with its equivalent in Acts) reflects one distinctive concern of his gospel, to put Jesus within the context of history. The dates he periodically gives fulfil the same function (e.g. 1.5; 2.1,2; 3.1). This is a story that really happened on the stage of world history, and it has implications for world history from now on. The opening paragraph refers to a gentile reader, Theophilus, who is perhaps interested in the Christian faith but not yet quite committed to it. Nevertheless, Luke, like Matthew, writes from the perspective of the church.

One of his ways of reflecting this is his periodic references to the Holy Spirit, the one who brought the presence and the power of God and of Christ to Christians who lived after Christ's death and resurrection. Another is his interest in the subject of prayer: he refers often to Jesus's prayer-life and tells more than the other gospels of his teaching on the subject.

As is fitting for the work that is to be continued (in Acts) in the story of the spread of the gospel through the world, Luke, even in the story of Jesus's ministry, emphasizes his concern for the outcast (in parables such as the Pharisee and the Tax Collector, 18.9–14, and stories such as Zacchaeus in 19.1–9), the lost (in the parables in chapter 15 about the lost sheep, the lost coin, and the lost son), and the Samaritans (e.g. the story of the 'Good Samaritan' in chapter 10). Luke alone tells of the mission of the seventy-two disciples (10.1–18).

But what most distinguishes Luke's gospel is the fact that it is only Part One of a two part work. The Acts of the Apostles is his Part Two, as its opening verses show. Luke, like the other Christians, believed that the coming of Jesus meant that 'the last days' had dawned (Acts 2.17). But this did not mean that the whole story of how God's purpose was achieved was over. It was continued in the story of the church. Jesus had declared that his followers were to bear witness to him through the whole world – in Jerusalem, in all of Judaea and Samaria, and to the ends of the earth (Acts 1.8). Thus Acts shows first how the gospel began to triumph in Jerusalem (chapters 1–7) and spread through Palestine (chapters 8–12), both especially through the ministry of Peter. This latter section tells of the conversion of Saul/Paul and of the first Gentiles, and from now on attention is transferred from Peter to Paul, who carries the torch around the eastern Mediterranean and eventually as far as Rome itself. The programme set by Jesus is thus implemented with the power, inspiration, and guidance of the Spirit. God's own involvement is indicated by the ironies that Saul, the chief persecuter, becomes Paul, the most energetic missionary; and the Jews and the Romans unwittingly combine to make it possible for him to preach the gospel at the capital of the empire. In fact, the story is not so much of the Acts of the Apostles as of the Acts of the Holy Spirit; or rather, of some of the Acts of the Holy Spirit, for the story of the first years of the church was a much broader one than is covered by Acts. Nevertheless the account of how the church spread from Jerusalem to Rome is fundamental to the history of the church from then on.

JOHN

The fourth gospel is a different world again. Gone is the rapid succession of quickly sketched scenes around Galilee, the successions of parables and miracle-stories. John offers us a score of more carefully written, worked-out units, mostly against the background of Jerusalem. Perhaps his picture corresponds to what he had seen and heard there himself; perhaps it is a version elaborated as a result of his meditation and preaching over the years. A simple scene becomes the occasion or jumping-off point, often by means of conversation between Jesus and his hearers, for a long discussion of the issues involved in his ministry. They are simple scenes, but often 'mighty works'. The stories are vivid: one can easily imagine the panic at Cana when the drink ran out (chapter 2), or the discreet visit of the uncomprehending Nicodemus who cannot quite make Jesus out (chapter 3), or Jesus's uninhibited conversation with a much-married foreigner at Jacob's well (chapter 4). A thread of gentle humour runs through the stories too, often at the expense of the luckless Pharisees (derided by the ordinary folk whose blind son Jesus had healed (chapter 9), because they were unable to explain the phenomenon), sometimes in the description of the almost equally uncomprehending disciples (such as the lugubrious Thomas (11.16): 'Let's go to Jerusalem and die with him').

Humour, pathos and tragedy go together, however. Peter, challenged by Jesus as to whether the disciples will stick by him, opens his heart full of deep doubt and deep commitment:

'Lord, to whom would we go? You have the words that give eternal life' (6.68). The incomprehension of the Jewish leaders is amusing, but it is also culpable and, in a sense demonic. The polemic against 'religiousness' without personal response to Jesus is stronger here than anywhere else in the Bible.

The stories are memorable, and so are the sayings. In particular, in John, there recur Jesus's 'I am's' – the bread of life (6.35), the light of the world (8.12), the gate for the sheep (10.7), the good shepherd (10.11), the resurrection and the life (11.25), the way, the truth, and the life (14.6), the real vine (15.1). Each of these constitutes a claim to recognition as the only one who can really meet men's needs, and an invitation to respond to him and prove him as such. The 'I am's' are one of the marks of the more exalted picture of Jesus the Son of God which characterizes this gospel.

At the beginning of his gospel John speaks of Christ as 'the Word' – God's way of expressing himself – and the stories show him as the revelation of God. At the end, Thomas acknowledges him as 'my Lord and my God' (20.28). In John's gospel, Jesus speaks much more openly and systematically about his relationship with his Father. He also speaks more of the personal relationship between himself and his Father on the one hand, and those who believe in him on the other; a relationship to be developed by the coming of the Holy Spirit to the disciples after Jesus's departure. But the Jesus of John's gospel is also pictured in his humanity as clearly as anywhere in the Bible: tired, thirsty, weeping, troubled, questioning. John's statement of his purpose in writing indicates that he aimed to lead his readers to the belief that this Jesus (the figure of history) is the Christ, the Son of God (20.31).

The word of God to his people

In the Bible, God is the God who acts; this is a major theme of the 'story' we have been looking at so far. In the overall outworking of world history, in the story of Israel, in the coming of Christ, and in the life of individuals, God is at work.

But in the Bible, God is also the God who speaks. From Jeremiah's day comes a threefold summary of the ways by which people expected to hear God speak to them: 'There will always be priests to instruct us, wise men to give us counsel, and prophets to proclaim God's message' (Jeremiah 18.18). Subsequent to Jeremiah's day there developed two further means by which this word came. In the New Testament, the apostles in their letters directed the people of God, in a way in some respects analogous to the earlier role of the prophets. And towards the end of both Testaments there appear books (Daniel and Revelation) which are more visionary, and which claim to reveal the secrets of the end, when God's purpose will finally be brought to fulfilment.

9

The law of the priests:

Exodus to Deuteronomy

EXODUS

The law is connected with the priests in two senses. First, it was to the priest that a man would go for a ruling on a point of law. The priest was the expert in God's law, who could pronounce authoritatively concerning questions one might want to ask. Thus Jesus sent a cleansed leper to the priests (Luke 17.14) to fulfil the prescribed procedures required of someone who was to be regarded as restored to the normal life of the community. The law was entrusted to the levitical priests for the purpose of teaching the people (Deuteronomy 31.9; 33.10).

Clearly on many occasions, however, the law would contain no regulation that precisely covered the inquiry made of it, and it seems likely that the laws in the Old Testament partly accumulated through the growth of case law. A priest was asked a question about a difficult problem or a special case, and he (and his colleagues, no doubt) sought to establish what ruling was in accord with the mind of God and with the truth of God as they already knew it.

In particular examples of laws, one can see the modification of bare principles which may have come about in this way. Thus Exodus 21 offers the general principle that a man is not to be held guilty of a capital offence if his ox kills someone (verse 28). But what if the animal has killed before? Then he is guilty (verses 29–30). What if the animal gores a child? The same rules apply (verse 31). What if it gores a slave? Compensation is to be paid to the slave's owner (verse 32).

On other occasions, we are offered the bare general principle. Many of the ten commandments exemplify these laws: they simply look Israel in the eye and declare 'there is to be no stealing', and so on. No special cases are specified; Israel is challenged to apply the laws in a sensible way to her life. No sanctions are declared; to say 'if you do that I'll . . .' weakens the force of the commandment by implying that we assume it will be disobeyed.

Although the *torah* connects the law with Moses, and we can see the law being taught and developed through the priesthood, it is clear that its origins lay much further back. Many of its provisions make sense, for instance, against the background of the clan life of the time before Moses. Many other laws have parallels in the law codes of other ancient peoples. The best known example of this is the law code of Hammurabi, five centuries older than the time of Moses. These were, no doubt, the kind of laws that characterized the civilization from which the patriarchs came, as well as that of the Canaanites among whom the later Israelites lived.

Although the *torah* includes many close parallels with these laws, the Israelite versions have distinctive tendencies of their own. They are often more humanitarian; stealing is not a capital offence, as it was even in eighteenth century Britain, and there is no mutilation of criminals by cutting off hands or feet. On the other hand, sometimes Israel's laws are more strict: adultery is punished by death. So, of course, is murder; for man is made in God's image, and to attack God's image is to attack God. Israel's laws are more egalitarian: there is not one law for the rich, another for the poor. Indeed, they emphasize that justice is due to the weak. They are interested in compensation as well as punishment: there is no penalty for hurting someone in a fight, but you do have 'to pay for his lost time and take care of him until he gets well' (Exodus 21.19).

It is possible, then, to claim the superiority of these laws at some points. But they will also seem to us sometimes less enlightened than state law of our own day. The acceptance of slavery and the lower position of women strike us, now that slavery is assumed to be wrong and women are assumed to have the same rights as men. The Old Testament laws start from where the people of their culture were. They are not a revelation of unrealizable ideals, but a collection of attempts to make life a little more humanitarian than it might otherwise be.

LEVITICUS

The law is the business of priests. Very obviously their concern are the laws about worship which are concentrated in Leviticus. In moving on from the laws in Exodus, we move from what we might think of as a statute book to a prayer book. Yet religious questions appear throughout the books of law. The Israelites made no sharp distinction between criminal law, social custom, moral precept and cultic rubric. They aimed to bring the whole of life under the lordship of God. Nevertheless, the perspective of Leviticus is that of the requirements of religion. Here are put into writing the regulations regarding different types of sacrifice (chapters 1–7) which were of great importance in a situation in which sacrifice was the way by which the relationship between God and man was expressed and restored. Five chapters (11–15) of rules describe what causes 'uncleanness' and how it can be dealt with. These regulations reflect various concerns, including hygiene and social order, but the most basic is probably a desire to outline ways in which Israel can show that she is no ordinary nation but one that is somehow different. These chapters lie behind the kosher laws which still distinguish the Jews.

However, one of the most striking of the laws lying behind kosher practices appears not in Leviticus but in Exodus (twice) and Deuteronomy: 'Do not cook a young sheep or goat in its mother's milk' (Exodus 23.19; 34.26; Deuteronomy 14.21). Perhaps this unlikely-sounding barbarism was practised in Canaanite religion; its background is obscure. But this law has had great influence, for it was interpreted by the rabbis as a command that meat and milk should never be cooked in the same vessels or consumed in the same meal. So, because of this law, every El Al airliner today carries two kitchens with two sets of utensils, and (until the recent invention of an artificial 'milk') served only black coffee after a meat meal.

The later laws in Leviticus (chapters 17–26) are more mixed:

some concern ritual questions, others are directly ethical. But running through them is a concern for Israel's holiness: 'You are to be holy, because I, the Lord your God, am holy' (19.2). This motivation is mentioned in connection with all sorts of laws; evidently to be holy is to be set apart, to be different. Here is made explicit the concern mentioned above: Israel is called to be distinctive, and thereby to witness to the distinctiveness of her God.

Leviticus here includes one of the accounts of Israel's religious festivals (chapter 23). The list actually begins with the sabbath, a weekly day of rest and worship. The ten commandments (Exodus 20 and Deuteronomy 5) suggest two reasons for the observance of the sabbath: it is an imitation of God in his creative activity (for he worked for six days and then rested); and it is a reminder of the mercy shown by God to the Israelites in Egypt (for as slaves there, they had no opportunity to rest). Sabbath observance became a distinctive mark of an Israelite in the exile, as we noted in chapter 4.

The sabbath principle is later extended (chapter 25) to the giving of a sabbath, or fallow, year to agricultural land. Then one sabbath year in seven was a 'year of restoration' when debts were cancelled. Land that had been sold was returned to its original owner, and slaves were freed. The land belongs to God and, under God, to the families to whom he had allocated it (in the time of Joshua), so it cannot be sold; and people are made in God's image, so they cannot be 'possessed'.

The list of actual festivals begins with Passover, in March/April. The Israelites were told to make this feast the beginning of their year (Exodus 12), for it marked the event which constituted their beginning as a nation (see chapter 4 above). It is characteristic of Israel's religious festivals that they have a background both in the life of the farmer or the shepherd and in the history of the redemption of God's people – rather as Christmas and Easter are christian festivals with pagan elements. The ceremony of Passover involved killing a lamb and daubing its blood on the door-posts of the house. This practice probably had its background in the annual cycle of the life of a nomadic shepherd. But the exodus from Egypt happened at the time of this festival. It became part of the event of the exodus (Exodus chapters 11–13) and part of the story of God's salvation of his people. It was at the time of Passover that Jesus was killed; thus Easter and Passover come at the same time of year. The New Testament sees Jesus's death as like the death of the Passover lamb, which made redemption possible.

Passover is accompanied by the first of the agricultural festivals, Unleavened Bread, when the old year's leaven was thrown out in anticipation of new crops. In terms of the exodus story, the practice of eating unleavened bread recalls the haste of the Israelites' departure from Egypt, which left no time for using yeast and waiting for the bread to rise! (Exodus 12.39).

The importance of Israel's agricultural life is indicated by the fact that she celebrated several harvest festivals. These began with the commencement of the corn harvest. The first sheaf to be gathered was taken to the priest (Leviticus 23.10); in other areas of life, too, the principle was accepted that the firstfruits went to God. The farmer gave to God the first animal each mother bore (Exodus 13.12). Even the firstborn of a human mother was God's by right (Exodus 13.2). Other nations actually sacrificed firstborn children to the gods, and so did Israelites in times of religious and moral degradation. But the old story of Abraham and Isaac (Genesis 22) records that, while the willingness to make this great sacrifice is valued, the child is to be replaced at God's instruction by an animal.

Seven weeks after the offering of the first sheaf, the completion of the corn harvest was celebrated, at Pentecost. Here Leviticus breaks out of its concern with worship to note that at harvest the edges of the fields are to be left so that poor people and foreigners who have no land of their own to harvest, may help themselves.

Before the final harvest festival came two other occasions. The calendar year began (as it still does in Israel) in September/October, 'the seventh month' if you reckon from Passover. This is the beginning of the agricultural year: the rains are due to come after the long drought of summer. Nature will be able to come to life again, and ploughing for the next year's crop will be possible. The beginning of the year is celebrated by a special day of rest and worship; lesser celebrations were included to mark the beginning of each month.

Ten days later comes the most solemn day of the year, *Yom Kippur*, the Day of Atonement, 'when the annual ritual is to be performed to take away the sins of the people' (Leviticus 23.26–7). The ritual itself (chapter 16) involved first sacrificing a goat in the temple; then the high priest laid hands on another goat, an act which symbolized the transfer to it of the people's sins, before driving it off into the desert. The ceremony symbolized Israel's awareness that wilful sin has to be dealt with, though driving it away into the desert may not seem a finally satisfactory solution.

The Day of Atonement was in turn followed by a final great occasion of joy, celebrating the full gathering in of the harvest. It was called 'the Festival of Shelters' and recalled not only the practice of sleeping out of doors in makeshift bivouacs during the harvest, but also the necessity of living in these 'simple shelters' after the people left Egypt.

DEUTERONOMY

We have said something about Deuteronomy in chapter 5. Here is the most systematic exposition of God's requirements of his people within the covenant. The book begins by making it clear that God is not interested in a merely outward response to what he has done for them. He wants to be their only God; he wants the love of heart, soul and strength (6.4–5). Jesus took this as the foremost of the commandments (Matthew 22.37); the second most important was the command from Leviticus (19.18) that one should love one's neighbour as one loves oneself. To every Jew, these verses are the centre of his creed, the ones he recalls most often.

Deuteronomy goes on to itemize the personal response God looks for from his people: trust in him, reverence for him, loyalty to him. They are continually to recall the blessings he has shown to them. And they are to give concrete expression to their response in detailed obedience to his laws. The content of these laws is similar to that of the laws of Exodus, Leviticus and Numbers. If there is something distinctive in Deuteronomy, it is the systematization of the Lord's demands. Chapters 12–26 cover almost every conceivable aspect of the life of the people of God: worship, mourning practices, food, giving, the treatment of slaves, festivals, the administration of justice, the conduct of war, the detection of crime, sexual purity, divorce and remarriage. The whole of life, corporate and individual, is to be brought under the lordship of Yahweh, so that in every way Israel can embody what it means to be 'the Lord's own people'.

The theology of Deuteronomy is beautifully balanced: grace and law, God's act and man's response, inner attitude and outward practice, the call to obedience and the warning of punishment, are finely set in relation to one another. But the law demands what cannot be given. The heyday of Deuteronomy was the reform of Josiah (see p. 53). But this reform was a failure. There was nothing wrong with the law. But there was something wrong with the men to whom it was given. It would have to be written on their hearts, not merely on stone tablets, before they would obey it (Jeremiah 31.33). Or, as Deuteronomy itself puts it, God will have to *give* them obedient hearts so that they will love him (30.6).

Neverthless, as we have noted already, the Jews do not see the law as a burden. It is the gracious gift of God, and fulfilling it is a way of responding to him. The law is thus a source of joy for a Jew. Even today one of the most joyous occasions of the Jewish year is the feast of 'Rejoicing in the Law'. This rejoicing features in the Old Testament in the lyrical joy in the law shown by some of the psalms (especially 119, with its 176 verses of enthusiasm over the law).

Admittedly the New Testament offers an entirely different attitude to law. There, it is because of their attachment to the law that the Jews reject Jesus their messiah. Attachment to the law has become legalism. They think that obeying the law earns them God's favour. An enthusiasm about the law, if it is not to go astray, has to recall that keeping God's commandments is not a way of earning a relationship with God. The relationship is given, and obedience is a response.

10

The word of the prophets:

Isaiah to Malachi

Fifteen books in the Bible, between Isaiah and Malachi, are named after prophets. In English Bibles (including GNB), Lamentations and Daniel also come in this section of the Bible; but they do not come here in the Hebrew Bible, and I am leaving them to chapters 13 and 14.

In the Hebrew Bible, the story from Joshua to Kings is regarded as part of the prophets, and this reflects an important feature about prophecy: it is essentially tied up with history. The prophets believed they brought a message direct from God, a message which reflected God's involvement in and lordship over the history of their day.

The heyday of prophecy is the time when Israel had kings – the time from Saul to the exile (and for a while after the exile, when there was some hope of a re-establishment of the monarchy). The significance of this fact is that the kings were always in danger of ruling in a way that ignored the fact that God was the real king of Israel. The prophets could speak a word of God which confronted the institutional leadership of the state. They could be the means of God's will being declared when the kings were opposed to God's will. We can see this happening with figures such as Samuel, Nathan, Ahijah, Elijah, Elisha, Amos, Isaiah and Jeremiah.

Evidently something new occurs in the eighth century with the appearance of Amos, Hosea, Isaiah and Micah; for the first time prophets have books named after them which collect their teaching and sometimes relate incidents from their lives. These prophets are no longer merely figures in the story related in

Samuel and Kings: indeed, only Isaiah and Jonah are mentioned there (Haggai and Zechariah do appear in Ezra).

Admittedly, it is probable that not everything in each book was actually uttered by the prophet whose name appears at the head of the first chapter. It is not quite that the books are anthologies, but that the original sayings of a prophet have sometimes been added to by his followers, who believed God was leading them to bring new messages to a later day but in the spirit of the great prophet to whom they looked back. The clearest example of this is the book of Isaiah. Isaiah bade his disciples to 'guard and preserve the messages' that God gave him (8.16) until the time they were fulfilled. The exile, a century and a half later, formed the vindication of the darker side of these messages, and now there arose new prophets 'in the spirit of Isaiah' who declared that his message was fulfilled and who preached the new message they believed he would now bring. Consequently, their preaching is included within the book of Isaiah, rather than forming a separate book. We will look at this example in more detail later. Probably some of the other books (especially Jeremiah, Ezekiel, Micah and Zechariah) have also been expanded to a greater or lesser extent. We have here, then, not merely the message of one prophet in one century, but the additional messages of further prophets which bring the word of God to a later age.

But why did these prophets, beginning in the eighth century, come to have books named after them at all? With Amos something new came into Israel's religion. Until his day, the events which fundamentally decided Israel's faith had been events of the past – the events from Abraham through the exodus and conquest of Palestine to the establishment of the monarchy, the capture of Jerusalem, and the building of the temple. Amos, however, declares that the event of which Israel has to take most account is still to come: it is the day of the Lord. Furthermore, there is a radicalism about the message of these prophets which goes beyond merely turning Israel round to face the future instead of the past. They also declare that the future will be unpleasant. This day of the Lord will be darkness, not light (Amos 5.18–20). It means, in fact, the end of life as Israel knows it, unless she turns from her moral unrighteousness, her social injustice, her religious unfaithfulness and her political pragmatism.

The prophets were thus both fore-tellers and forth-tellers. They declared events that were to take place: when Israel was characterized by sinfulness and self-confidence they declared judgement, when her faith and morale had gone (in the exile) they brought a message of future restoration. In this sense they were foretellers. However, they were not soothsayers nor merely men who could read the signs of the times. Often their message went against what was politically likely; it was based on what they believed God told them, a revelation checked by considering what was morally demanded even if not politically inevitable.

But as well as speaking of the future, they proclaimed God's demands of the present moment. A key word which recurs is 'repentance' or 'turning'. The people have *turned* away from God and they risk him *turning* away from them unless they *turn* back Repentance is not a mere feeling of sorrow but a redirection of the whole person. God's demand is that, in the light of what the prophet says about the future, they should turn round their lives in the present.

In speaking thus, they saw themselves as God's 'messengers'. An earthly king had messengers to make his pronouncements. The messengers would say, 'The king says, inasmuch as such-and-such is the case, I declare that such-and-such will happen.' Similarly the prophet declares, 'The *Lord* says, inasmuch as such-and-such is the case (his people have rebelled against him), I declare that such-and-such will happen (they will go into exile).' But he uses all sorts of means to get his point home: he declares a curse on the people (like a man cursing another man), he laments the people's unfaithfulness (like a man sorrowing over the unfaithfulness of his wife), he sings a dirge over the doomed nation (like the mourners at a funeral), he tells parables and riddles to get attention and then to capitalize on it – in every way to try to drive home the crucial message he has been given.

It is worth trying to appreciate the outward form of these

different types of message. All the individual examples have their distinctive points: but there is something to learn from the outward shape that they often have in common. This point may be appreciated if we consider how we ourselves learn a lot simply from the outward form and shape of things that we read. We may receive, for instance, several different types of letter: one typed on headed notepaper from a business concern, another handwritten, another printed. The language they use may differ: formal and legal, personal and friendly, or the enthusiastic superlatives of an advertising circular. Before we read the specific message, we know 'how' to read it: what allowances to make for exaggeration, what to read between the lines. Then we find that, when (for instance) an advertising circular is written in the form of a personal letter or of a consumer report, it achieves (or it hopes to achieve) a different kind of impact.

Similarly, the prophets achieved different kinds of impact by taking up the varied speech forms of everyday life and utilizing them for their religious purpose.

Quite often the prophets did not merely preach the message – they acted it out. A classic example is Jeremiah breaking a clay jar (Jeremiah 19). This was not merely a piece of drama. Because Jeremiah was called by God and given God's words, he was putting God's will into effect. His breaking the jar was, as it were, setting the wheels in motion for the breaking up of the state. Indeed, even without such a piece of dramatic symbolism, there was power in the prophet's words. They were bound to come true, in so far as he was called by God. Thus efforts were often made to shut the prophets up (see Jeremiah 20). They were dangerous men.

ISAIAH

The book of Isaiah falls into clear divisions.

1–12 Isaiah's indictments of the people of Judah in the time of King Ahaz. Judah is very religious but full of immorality and injustices; and in practice she does not trust her God but tries to protect herself against the Assyrians by deft political alliances with the Egyptians. Isaiah warns of God's judgement but promises that God will eventually restore her: the section ends with a psalm of praise for Israel to sing 'in that day'.

13–23 Isaiah declares that God's judgement will also fall on the other nations: Babylon, Moab, Damascus, Ethiopia, Egypt, Assyria, Dumah, Arabia, Tyre. Part of his indignation is, of course, grounded in the nations' opposition to Judah. But they are also seen as punished for their pride. And – to make it clear that her sin means she is in no better a position than anyone else – Jerusalem is included too.

24–27 Further pictures of judgement and restoration, but the references are less political and less specific. The picture is more one of final judgement and resurrection.

28–35 Indictments of Judah, warning of judgement but promising that God will eventually restore her, when, 'the desert will rejoice and flowers will bloom in the wilderness'. The chapters parallel 1–12, but the difference is that these messages belong to the reign of King Hezekiah, and the challenge to trust in God becomes the central feature.

36–39 reflect the same period, the reign of Hezekiah; these are not messages *of* Isaiah, however, but stories *about* Isaiah similar to those recorded in 2 Kings. They look beyond the reign of Hezekiah to the exile.

40–55 presuppose the exile has already happened and introduce an entirely new note: here 'comfort' to the distressed is the centre of the message. God is about to defeat the Babylonians and take this people back to Palestine.

56–66 are again less specific in reference. They are like 1–12 in that they challenge the people about their unrighteousness and disobedience; but they seem to reflect a much later situation in Palestine, when the return promised in 40–55 has been achieved but all is still not as it should be. The whole book closes with a promise of a new creation of heaven and earth.

Isaiah's vision of the holy one (chapter 6) lies behind the varied messages of the book.

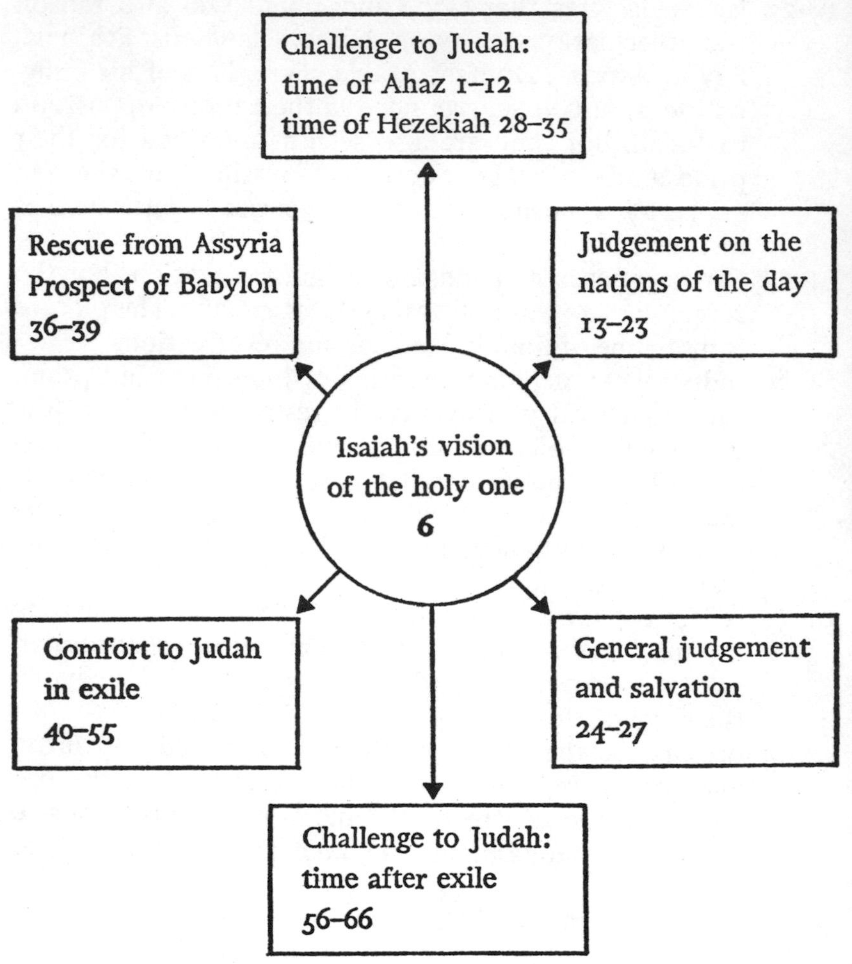

Isaiah is a man of Jerusalem, of the temple, and perhaps of the royal court. He knows that God committed himself to Jerusalem, that he chose Jerusalem as his city, that the temple in Jerusalem is his home, that the king who rules in Jerusalem is God's representative. On the other hand, he also knows that God is a God of justice and a 'jealous' God. He does not look lightly on men who are unfaithful to him. This places Isaiah in a dilemma. The social and moral life of Jerusalem is rotten through and through; therefore Jerusalem deserves judgement. The leaders of Judah fail to trust in God and instead implement the pragmatic policy of shrewd political deals with various nations around; therefore they deserve judgement. But this is God's city and the king is God's anointed.

Isaiah therefore declares that Jerusalem must be chastised, but it will not actually fall. At the crucial moment God will rescue his people from the invader and punish him. The kings must be chastised, but the line of David will not be cast off. Some of the passages that are used in church at Christmas time (Isaiah 7.14; 9.2–7; 11.1–5) express this promise of a king who will really live up to the Davidic ideal.

Another motif by means of which Isaiah reconciles God's faithfulness to Israel with the necessity of his punishing her is the idea of 'the few'. He calls his son 'A few will come back' (7.3). The phrase could suggest several ideas, in all of which Isaiah may have seen some truth. One is that only a few will escape the calamity God is bringing, and return to the promised land. The name is thus a message of judgement. But at the same time it could suggest a message of hope – 'at least, a few will come back'. In this sense, all will not be lost. The phrase then could refer to coming back in repentance to God (not merely physically returning to the land): it contains an implicit moral challenge as to whether the hearer belongs to 'the few'. Understood with various emphases, this idea of 'the few' was of lasting theological importance.

Isaiah's conviction that Judah must undergo a terrible chastisement probably derives from his experience of God's call (Isaiah 6). There in the temple, perhaps in the course of one of the great services when the congregation as a whole rejoiced in the presence of God, Isaiah had a new kind of experience, a vision of God himself, with his angels proclaiming 'holy, holy, holy', and the Lord himself appealing for someone to declare God's message of judgement to his people. The vision of God as 'the holy one' shaped Isaiah's ministry. His characteristic title for God is 'the holy one of Israel'. Because Israel's God is the holy one, she must be punished, even though she is his people.

The description of God as 'the holy one of Israel' recurs in the later parts of the book, and it thus forms a theme which holds together the book as a whole. In chapters 40–55 the fact that God is the holy one of Israel is no longer a threat but an encouragement. Israel is in exile, having undergone the punishment which the earlier chapters spoke of (and more). Now the prophet promises that the demoralized exiles can have their faith built up, because 'the holy one of Israel' is their redeemer.

As we noted in the first part of this chapter, however, a question that arises here is, 'who is the prophet who speaks in Isaiah 40–55?' At first sight, since the chapters belong to the same book as the earlier prophecies of Isaiah, it seems that these too, must be Isaiah's words. But the speaker seems actually to live in the exile. He does not merely predict exile and restoration, as Isaiah could certainly have done. He speaks of the exile as being in his day almost over. The natural inference is that these are the words of another prophet who lived at this later period; and the final chapters of the book (56–66) come from further prophets who ministered back in Palestine later still. All these prophets looked at matters from a similar perspective to that of Isaiah himself (and thus their work was included in the collection that bears his name). They were all prophets of 'the holy one of Israel'.

The author of chapters 40–55 is often spoken of as the 'second Isaiah'. Although he had many points in common with 'first Isaiah', he also has his own distinctive characteristics. One difference, the fact that his message is one of hope, not fundamentally of judgement, derives from his historical situation. But second Isaiah emphasizes the exodus – in the sense that the return from exile will be a new exodus even better than the first – whereas first Isaiah had not mentioned the exodus. Then, whereas first Isaiah had emphasized the Davidic king, second Isaiah does not speak of a Davidic messiah. Indeed he sees the whole people as now given the special relationship with God which once belonged to David (chapter 55). The people are called to be God's servant – though the prophet realizes that they cannot live up to this calling. One of the high points of the Old Testament is reached when second Isaiah depicts what the calling of God's servant involves. It demands the acceptance of suffering and affliction; but God promises that such acceptance can bear fruit, because it will be the means of reconciling God and man.

JEREMIAH

The book of Jeremiah cannot be divided into sections in the clear way that the book of Isaiah can – though chapters 1–25 are mostly concerned with the teaching of Jeremiah, 26–45 with stories about Jeremiah, 46–51 with his indictments of other nations (these are similar to Isaiah 13–23), and 52 is a tailpiece that repeats the story which appears at the end of 2 Kings of how Jerusalem is taken (and Jeremiah's prophecies are thereby proved true).

The presence of so many stories about Jeremiah is one striking feature about the book. There are very few comparable stories in the books of the other prophets. Jeremiah begins by telling us how he came to be called to be a prophet (the story of his call provides the justification for the ministry he goes on to exercise). He tells us about many events in his ministry, for instance about some of the occasions on which he received a message from God (e.g. on a visit to a pottery, chapter 18) and on which he delivered a message of God (e.g. in the temple, chapter 25). Frequently, the stories relate what reaction Jeremiah's message received, and here lies their significance. Jeremiah may have been no more successful than other prophets (the prophets were usually failures), but the personal opposition he received was, as far as we know, sharper than that shown to any other prophet. The stories about him are stories of how he is thrown in the stocks, threatened with death, imprisoned in an empty water cistern, mocked by other prophets. Jeremiah brings God's message; but what people think of God's message is expressed in what they do to the messenger.

Outside the stories about Jeremiah, the same point lies behind those sections of Jeremiah's poems in which he pours out his heart to God with a frankness and urgency unparalleled in the Bible (chapters 11–20). These 'confessions of Jeremiah' tell us the inward story of his sufferings, of the cost that being a prophet brought to him personally. In the case of Jeremiah, God's message and God's messenger become hard to distinguish. Jeremiah is identified with God; so how men treat Jeremiah expresses what they think of God.

There are parallels between Jeremiah's message and that of Isaiah a century before: both declared that judgement must

---

JEREMIAH 1–25: JEREMIAH'S MESSAGE

1 His call

2–6 Judah's apostasy and immorality, and its punishment

7–10 Further warnings, emphasizing the danger of false trust in the temple (7), in the word (8), and in idols (10)

11–20 The rejection of God's message and the persecution of God's messenger

21–24 Further warnings from the time of Zedekiah

25 His review of his 23 years of ministry from his call to 604

26–35 *The demand of God's message (i)*

26–29 Three parallel narratives emphasizing that the more stubbornly people resisted Jeremiah's message, the worse their trouble

30–33 But the darkest hour is the dawn of hope: God does not intend judgement to be the end

34–35 The choice: to be like the nation, which continues to rebel and must be judged (34), or to be like the few who keep their commitments (35)

36–45 *The demand of God's message (ii)*

36 Introduction: the task given to Baruch, and the challenge given through him, to respond to God's message

37–44 Four scenes from the story of the fall of Jerusalem, the events which followed the fall, and Jeremiah's enforced departure to Egypt. Each scene (37–38; 39–41; 42–43; 44) depicts the Jews offered a new start if they will accept God's will. But each time the chance is lost as the people continue to resist.

45 Conclusion: the cost for Baruch, and the challenge given to him, to remain faithful even if he is alone

come on the people of God. But there are important differences, which arise in part out of their background. Isaiah was a man at home in Jerusalem and used to thinking of it as God's dwelling-place. Thus he saw clearly that God was committed to Jerusalem and to the Davidic kings, and he promised that God would rescue Jerusalem and be faithful to his promise to David.

Isaiah was proved right; Jerusalem escaped by a miracle from the attacks of King Sennacherib. Isaiah's message was, in fact, vindicated too well. Men came to trust too confidently in the eternal security of Jerusalem. Thus, when in Jeremiah's day Jerusalem came under pressure again (this time from the Babylonians), there were plenty of prophets prepared to reiterate Isaiah's message: to say that Jerusalem would be safe because God would look after it. Their preaching could be backed up by the claim that, after all, Judah had reformed herself (in the reign of King Josiah): therefore God was bound to be on her side.

Thus Jeremiah had to dissent from some very strong and plausible theological lines. The reform of Josiah was not enough, he declared (though he probably himself supported it when Josiah initiated it): the evils of men's hearts had not been changed by the external measures that Josiah had imposed. The message of Isaiah, applicable though it may have been in Isaiah's day, was inappropriate now.

Jeremiah was the man to deliver this message because he was a very different man from Isaiah. He was not a Jerusalemite. He came from a village, Anathoth, only a few kilometres north of Jerusalem, but across the crucial boundary between the tribal areas of Judah and Benjamin. He belonged, therefore, to the north rather than to the south. His kinsfolk would not be orientated to Jerusalem. This was still more the case if we are right to assume that the priestly family to which he belonged (1.1) was the one which had been excluded from the Jerusalem priesthood in the time of Solomon (1 Kings 2).

The northern tribes were naturally less interested in Jerusalem than Judah was, and they were, consequently, apparently more attentive to the earlier theology of the exodus and the covenant. The exodus is not mentioned in prophets such as Isaiah and Micah – God's choice of Jerusalem and David is everything. It is the northern prophets who speak of the exodus faith. And Jeremiah, though he preaches in Jerusalem, is a northern prophet. Thus he calls Jerusalem back to the faith which lay behind God's choice of Jerusalem and David, the earlier story of God's making of his covenant with Israel in the time of Moses. It was a story which laid great emphasis on the moral, social and political implications of a relationship with Yahweh (Isaiah, of course, had been aware of these) and declared that judgement, and specifically exile, would come upon those who did not take the exodus faith seriously.

It was perhaps inevitable that Judah should prefer the comfortable message of her own prophets, based on the earlier messages of their great predecessor Isaiah, to the strange indictments of this nervous young man from across the border.

Not that Jeremiah's picture is all darkness. He, too, includes those prophecies against the nations which are indirectly a comfort to Judah. He also explicitly promises that the other side of judgement there is hope (chapters 30–33). The covenant is finished – but God will make a new one, when man's deep moral problem will be solved by the writing of the law on men's hearts, the reforming of their characters from the inside. The exodus is to be undone by an exile – but then there will be a new exodus to outshine the first one and make it not worth speaking of. The Davidic monarchy is doomed – but then it will be re-established, with kings to live up to their names (Zedekiah means 'Yahweh is my righteousness', but he ignored Yahweh's claims. Jeremiah promises that there is going to be a king called 'Yahweh is our righteousness').

Jeremiah puts his money where his mouth is. At the height of the siege of Jerusalem, he agreed to buy a plot of land in Anathoth. Humanly speaking, it was a laughable gesture: what use is owning land when an enemy is taking over the whole country? But Jeremiah believed that God was bringing judgement and God would bring restoration; the time for cultivating land would come again. A prophet always confronts his people's attitudes. When they are confident, he issues warnings. When the moment of despair comes, it is the time for a message of hope.

EZEKIEL

Ezekiel's ministry coincided with the later part of that of Jeremiah – the years just before and just after the fall of Jerusalem (587 BC). But he prophesied in Babylon, not in Jerusalem, so we never see the two of them together. Ezekiel was among the first groups of Jews to be taken into exile after Nebuchadnezzar's first siege of Jerusalem (597). His calling then in Babylon was to prepare his fellow-Jews for the worse calamity that was still to come.

Like the Jews left in Judaea, the Jews taken into exile in 597 could not believe that the city would ever be destroyed. They assumed that their exile would be a short one and that they would soon be back home. Exekiel's task was to keep repeating that, because of the Jews' unfaithfulness to their God, it was inevitable that a worse judgement should come.

The first half of the book of Ezekiel (chapters 1–24) reiterates this message which Ezekiel preached between 597 and 587. In the arrangement of the book, the transition to a more encouraging message begins with chapters 25–32, where Ezekiel declares that God's judgement will fall on the other nations, too. They are especially condemned for their personal hostility and vindictiveness towards Israel. But the explicit good news for Israel begins in chapter 33. News arrives from Jerusalem that the city has finally fallen and the temple has been destroyed. At the moment of disaster Ezekiel's message changes. Now that the warning of judgement has been fulfilled, the way to restoration and blessing is open. God will give Israel leaders who lead her in the right way, he will recreate her from within, he will bring back to life the corpse she has become, he will win a final great victory over evil, he will rebuild her temple and come to dwell among her people again (chapters 33–48).

The way Ezekiel describes both Judah's sin and the nature of God's restoration of her reflects his own background. Like Jeremiah he comes from a priestly family; but unlike Jeremiah he belongs to the official priesthood of Jerusalem. His cast of mind is that of a priest. When he pictures the sin of Jerusalem, it is the sin of Israel's worship, the temple defiled by false worship. When he pictures God's judgement, it is in terms of the Lord's glory leaving the temple. When he pictures restoration, it is in terms of the building of a new and glorious temple.

But Ezekiel is no ordinary priest. He is a man of extraordinary personality. With Ezekiel everything is larger than life, three-dimensional, quadraphonic, full-frontal. At nearly every point, he is like the other prophets, only more so. He begins by telling of his call: but his story of his call is twice as long as anyone else's, a fantastic vision of the throne of God and a voice from heaven summoning him to eat a scroll full of declarations of judgement. He acts out in parabolic dramas the coming siege of Jerusalem (chapter 4) and the departure of further refugees from the city. He is transported in a vision back to the temple itself (chapter 8) and describes the enormities of the idolatrous worship offered there. He relates complex allegorical indictments of the wanton whoring of Jerusalem, the bride of God (chapter 16). But then the same range of gifts is used to paint the picture of a more glorious future: the valley of dry bones (just how Israel feels – chapter 37), the battle with Gog and Magog (38–39), the new temple with its stream of living water bringing life wherever it flows –

EZEKIEL

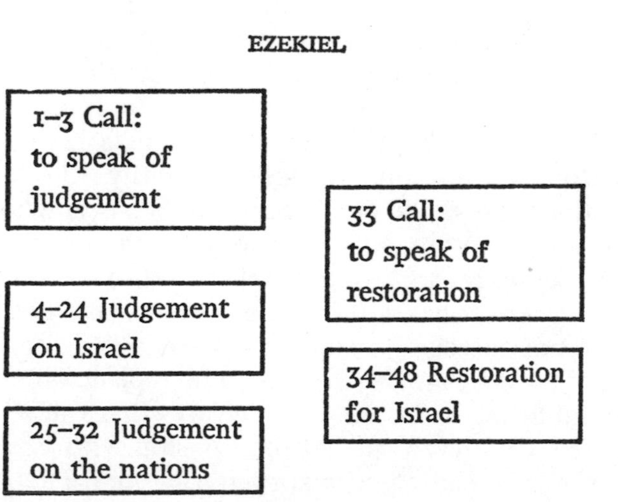

so that even the Dead Sea abounds in fish (40–47), the repossessed land, and the city now called 'The-Lord-is-Here!' (48.35).

The pictures are exciting. But have they ever come true? The nation was reformed, the land repossessed, the temple rebuilt, and so on, when some of the exiles were allowed to return to Palestine by the Persians. But it was a half-hearted affair, by no means as grand as the vision suggested by Ezekiel. The New Testament sees some of the promises given by Ezekiel as in a sense fulfilled through Jesus the messiah. He is the one from whom living waters flow (John 7.38). It sees other aspects of the picture of the new temple as suggesting something of the nature of heaven and of the 'new Jerusalem' (Revelation 21–22). Some Christians have seen Ezekiel as predicting events of our own day, or events soon to come (such as battles between Russia and America), but this seems fanciful.

THE TWELVE SHORTER PROPHETIC BOOKS

The Old Testament closes with twelve books often called 'the minor prophets'. The title is unfortunate, because it suggests that they are not very important, whereas actually they are, page for page, at least as important as the longer books which precede them! Possibly they were collected together because they conveniently fitted on one scroll, while Isaiah, Jeremiah, and Ezekiel each had a scroll of their own. Hosea comes first perhaps because it is the longest of the twelve; thereafter the order is mostly based on chronological considerations (see the chart opposite.)

Amos was a shepherd from Judah. He tells us that he did not come from a traditional prophetic family (there were professional prophets, like our professional clergy, whose job was to give advice, to preach, and so on). But he felt compelled by God to take up the task of a prophet, and to preach in the area of the northern tribes. His prophetic voice has a new tone to it. He does not merely give advice when asked for it, or even intervene to say that one king is to be replaced by another (as Elijah and Elisha had done). He declares that the whole nation is doomed. God has a special relationship with Israel, but this means she is specially guilty for ignoring him. There is a moral rigorousness about Amos that especially distinguishes him.

Hosea, too, prophesied in northern Israel, and the content of his message was similar: the state will be brought down by God. But the distinctive flavour of Hosea's message is provided by his insight into the love of God, which is as fundamental to God's character as is his holiness. Hosea knew in his own person the tension between love for his wife and rejection of her because she was unfaithful to him. He saw the same tension in God. Like Amos, he knew that God's holiness meant Israel had to be punished; and Amos and Hosea were proved right when the northern state was destroyed by the Assyrians (722). But both Amos and Hosea believed that, precisely because love lay behind it, judgement could not be God's last word, and they end on a note of hope.

THE PROPHETS

Eighth century	*Seventh century*	*Exile*	*Restoration*
Isaiah		(Isaiah 40–55)	(Isaiah 56–66)
	Jeremiah	Ezekiel	
Hosea	Nahum		Haggai
Amos	Habakkuk		Zechariah
Jonah (see chapter 7)	Zephaniah		Obadiah
			Malachi
Micah			
			Joel

Micah was a native of Judah who prophesied in Judah – like Isaiah, who has overshadowed him. His message is similar to Isaiah's, though he is perhaps more thoroughgoing in his declaration of judgement ('Zion will be ploughed like a field, Jerusalem will become a pile of ruins' – 3.12). The book of Micah has prophecies of judgement and restoration, following each other in two sets: chapter 1–3 and 4–5, then 6.1–7.6 and 7.7–20.

Nahum is concerned with the downfall of the empire of the Assyrians, epitomized by their capital city, Nineveh. Nineveh is seen as the Lord's opponent, as 'the lying, murderous city' (3.1), as an enchanting whore (3.4), as a cruel destroyer (3.19).

Habakkuk belongs to the same decades when the Babylonians are replacing the Assyrians as the dominant power of the middle east. Habakkuk is troubled by the injustice he sees all around him, and he asks what God is going to do about it. The Lord's response is to declare that he plans to use the up-and-coming Babylonians as his agents in punishing the wicked. Habakkuk is horrified: after all, the Babylonians deserve judgement themselves! God promises that their time will come. The book closes with a psalm of prayer for God to act.

Zephaniah, too, declares the punishment of both Judah and the nations on 'the day of the Lord', 'the day when God will act', 'the great day of the Lord'. But he looks beyond 'the day when the Lord shows his fury' to a day when the nations will turn to God and Judah will rejoice in the Lord being back with her.

Haggai prophesied at a time when judgement had come, and the exiled Jews had begun to return to their homeland. But life back in the promised land was not what they had hoped for, and they had abandoned trying to rebuild the temple. Haggai challenges men to make this their first priority; then they will know stupendous blessing, the fulfilment of the promise to re-establish David's house.

Zechariah, Haggai's contemporary, speaks to the same situation. He, too, challenges the Jews to keep up their commitment to God, but he lays greater emphasis on God's commitment to them. This is described in a series of visions: of the patrols reporting that all is quiet in the Persian empire (but

God is going to disturb this quiet in restoring Jerusalem), of four ox horns being crushed (thus will Judah's oppressors be shattered), of a man surveying Jerusalem with a view to rebuilding its walls (but the city will spread too fast to keep up with, and will be protected by God himself anyway), of the high priest accused but acquitted in heaven (God is restoring the temple worship), of a lampstand (symbolizing God's watching over the world), of an airborne scroll inscribed with a curse on perjury and robbery (which will be eliminated), of a woman carried off to Babylon (the removal of idolatry from Judah), of four more patrol chariots sent out to implement the Lord's will. The later chapters of Zechariah offer further pictures (puzzling in detail) of the restoration of Judah and punishing of the nations.

Obadiah declares that the Edomites, who were related to the Israelites but were their enemies, will be punished for their pride and cruelty to Israel. The Israelites will themselves rule Edom on the Lord's behalf.

Malachi reflects the same circumstances again as Haggai and Zechariah: discouragement at the hard conditions of the so-called restoration. Malachi calls on priests and people to honour God in their lives and worship, and warns them that 'the great and terrible day of the Lord' is coming – though for those who obey him, 'my saving power will rise on you like the sun and bring healing like the sun's rays' (4.1–2). Before that day, however, Elijah must come: the New Testament sees John the Baptist as fulfilling Elijah's role, while Jews to this day leave a place for Elijah at their Passover meal.

Joel is dominated by the picture of a plague of locusts. Locusts can completely destroy a country's food, and thus such a plague could mean total disaster. This calamity, then, speaks of the day of judgement, and Joel calls for repentance in the light of it. But he promises that God 'will restore what you lost in the years when swarms of locusts ate your crops' (2.23). A great day of judgement is still to come, but so is a great day of blessing, when God pours out his spirit on everyone (2.28).

11

The advice of the wise men:

Proverbs, Song of Songs

Nearly all the books we have looked at so far are very distinctively Jewish. The story of God and his people is the story of the Jews (even though at the beginning and end of the story the point is made that the God of Israel is also the God of the whole world). The law is the Jewish law; the Jews do not expect it to be kept by Gentiles. The prophets, even if they speak of the nations around, speak to the Israelite nation.

The advice of the wise men does not refer to the great events of Israel's history such as the exodus or the building of the temple; there is little distinctively Israelite about it. It is essentially concerned with life as it has to be lived every day by ordinary people. The wise men made it their business to try to understand what life was about by looking at it. They then say to us, this is how life works; if you want to be happy and successful, you will live in harmony with these facts of life.

Most of the advice comes in the form of maxims (the 'proverb' proper) just one verse long. They are collected in Proverbs 10–31 with very little concern for order. Sometimes they are prosaic and down-to-earth in their advice, but often they offer striking figures of speech which bring a smile with them: 'Beauty in a woman without good judgement is like a gold ring in a pig's snout' (11.22); 'It is better to meet a mother bear robbed of her cubs than to meet some fool busy with a stupid project' (17.12); 'The lazy man stays at home; he says a lion might get him if he goes outside' (22.13).

Yet the proverbs are not merely interested in the observation of life and with behaviour that pays. They are concerned with right behaviour (though they do believe that this is the same thing as behaviour that pays). Their moral exhortations are quite parallel to the laws of the *Torah*: e.g. 'Never move an old boundary-mark that your ancestors established' (17.28; cf. Deuteronomy 27.17).

Probably the parallels between the sayings of the wise men and the laws of the priests reflect a common background. Both are ultimately at home in the teaching of the family, and it may be that we should see their origin in the fatherly teaching given in the clan life of the patriarchs. This teaching was then passed on in the nation of Israel by two routes, via the priests and via the wise men.

The saying about the boundary-mark raises another issue. It is one of 'Thirty Wise Sayings' (see the heading at 22.17 in GNB) which appear in substantially the same form in an Egyptian work. Of all the Israelite writers, the wise men were the most open to learning from other peoples. Obviously other peoples could not write the story of Israel, but they could write of their own observation of life, and from this the Israelite wise men are willing to profit.

A third kind of learning and advice appears in the sayings of the wise men. As well as offering advice on what is sensible and on what is right, they talk about what is godly. Although they are trying to get as full a picture as possible of how life is and should be, they recognize that a total picture will inevitably elude them, for there remain enigmas about life. When we have done everything we can, we are still dependent on God: 'You can get horses ready for battle, but it is the Lord who gives victory' (21.31). 'A nation without God's guidance is a nation without order. Happy is the man who keeps God's law!' (29.18). Here the concern of the proverbs is close to that of the prophets, who sought to get Israel to take account of God's involvement in her life, to trust in him, and to pay attention to the demands of his will.

It would, indeed, be misleading to suggest that Proverbs only brings in God when it reaches the mysteries at the edge of human experience. Although the book is concerned with secular life, it does not take a secular approach. On the contrary, its belief in God underlies all its teaching. It examines the world, but it believes the world is God's – it reflects his mind, resulting as it does from his creative activity.

This point is made explicit in Proverbs 8.22–31, where God's own wisdom speaks and describes its (or her – Wisdom is personified as a woman in Proverbs) role as architect in God's creative work.

Like this paragraph, the other sections of the opening chapters of Proverbs (1–9) come in longer paragraphs than the one-verse couplets that characterize Proverbs 10–31. The earlier chapters also have a narrower range of interests, and two main themes recur. One is a repeated encouragement to take wisdom seriously – chapter 8 systematically expounds wisdom's invitation to pay attention. The other is a recurrent exhortation to avoid entanglement with other women. This second theme is entirely intelligible when understood in the straightforward sense. But why should it be given such prominence? Now in the prophets, sexual unfaithfulness is often a way of describing Israel's sin against the Lord, and it may well be that here in Proverbs the warning against unfaithfulness is an exhortation to stay committed to Yahweh – or perhaps to stay committed to wisdom; the two major themes of Proverbs 1–9 are then connected in this way. Wisdom is Yahweh's teaching. Young men are urged not to let their attention wander elsewhere.

THE SONG OF SONGS

We have noted above that the idea of faithfulness or unfaithfulness to God could be spoken of in terms of faithfulness or unfaithfulness to a human partner. In the Old Testament, Hosea makes this point in connection with his own marital experience, and in the New Testament Paul speaks of marriage as a picture of the relationship between Christ and his 'bride', the church (Ephesians 5.21–33).

Jews and Christians have valued the love poems in The Song of Songs as a reminder of the loving relationship that exists between the Lord and his people. They are written, however, as love poems, enthusing frankly over the beauty of the loved one and over the experience of the loving relationship. They have been described as an extended commentary on Genesis 2.18–25:

those verses describe the origin of the complementary relationship between man and woman, and these poems explore that God-created relationship.

'Song of Songs' means 'most beautiful of songs' (1.1). Similarly 'holy of holies' means 'most holy place', 'lord of lords' means 'supreme lord', and so on.

12

The letters of the apostles:

Romans to Jude

In some respects the 'epistles' (the word is merely an old one for letters) are the most surprising part of the Bible. They are a surprise because they are just letters. They are not sermons – though they include much exposition of scripture (that is, of the Old Testament) and instruction on Christian behaviour, and no doubt they were read out in church. They were not written as theological manuals (though they include much of the most profound theology in the Bible). Nor were they written with readers throughout the church in mind. They were part of a living relationship between certain people in particular situations during the first years of the life of the church.

So most of them begin like letters ('from Paul ... to the churches of Galatia: grace to you and peace ...') and end like letters ('signed: Paul') and pass on messages, and ask for greetings to be passed on to others and contain those snippets of information and comment which someone who is not inside the situation does not quite know how to take.

So why were they important enough to be included when the Christians collected their holy writings together?

Clearly the fundamental reason why the Christians held on to these letters was that they recognized that they dealt with important questions. They were not just the means of friends keeping in contact, or of someone getting a favour done by someone else (though they were that). They expressed the thinking of some very sharp minds on questions of religion and behaviour as these arose in the life of the early Christian church. Some, at least, were read out just like sermons in the services of the churches to which they were written. Sometimes they begin with a long section on the Christian faith, and then change the subject to questions of behaviour. Other letters interweave these two concerns all through. The combination of teaching on belief and behaviour is characteristic (as it was with the covenant in the Old Testament). Belief and behaviour are assumed to be linked closely together.

Even when they are discussing theology and ethics and church government, however, the letters remain rooted in particular situations. They are not theoretical manuals or systematic expositions of Christian truth. They are a series of responses to specific needs. This is most clear in a letter like 1 Corinthians, where Paul refers explicitly to the questions the Corinthians have asked him and the news about them that he has received. He gives them instruction on sexual morality because they have asked him certain questions; he describes how Christian worship should work because he has heard how theirs does not.

The 'occasional' nature of the theology of these letters appears in the way the points are expressed as well as in the subjects treated. This theology is not abstract and theoretical; it does not often talk in terms of 'the nature of reality' or 'the ground of being' or of 'two natures in one substance'. It characteristically expresses itself in picture language. This is particularly clear in the way the significance of Christ's dying for us is worked out. Being a Christian is like being declared innocent when you were guilty, being made free instead of being a slave, being admitted to the presence of a great king, being accepted as you are by someone who had a right to a grudge against you. Great theological words such as justification and redemption and atonement had their origin in the everyday life of non-Christian and Christian in the first century world.

So the fundamental reason why these letters were important was their content. But a second, and related, reason was their authorship, for they embody the teaching of the apostles. Except for Hebrews, they bear the names of apostles, or of others (such as Jesus's brother Jude) who could speak from experience of Jesus himself. And that is why these letters have more authority in the church than the profoundest theology that was to come later. They pass on an understanding of the significance of Jesus for the church as those who lived closest to him saw it.

It deserves mention, admittedly, that doubts have been raised about the authorship of a number of these letters. It has been suggested that, for instance, Peter's second letter was not written by Peter but was produced later by someone else who, perhaps, wanted to give expression to what Peter would have said if he were here now. Such a theory may seem an unlikely one, but it is difficult to disprove – though difficult to prove, too, and the content of these letters stands even if they were produced by someone other than the one named at the beginning.

Romans is Paul's longest letter, and his most systematic. It provides an outline of Paul's basic understanding of the gospel for the Christians in the capital of the empire, whom Paul

---

PAUL'S LIFE AND LETTERS

The dating of Paul's experiences and his letters is an uncertain matter. What follows is one *possible* scheme of *approximate* dates.

- 35 Conversion (Acts 9).
- 46–47 First missionary journey (Acts 13–14). From Antioch to Cyprus and Turkey, and back.
- 48–51 Second missionary journey (Acts 15–18). From Antioch through Turkey and Greece to Corinth – from here *1 and 2 Thessalonians* were written. Then back via Ephesus to Caesarea and Jerusalem.
- 53–58 Third missionary journey (Acts 18–21). From Antioch through Turkey to Ephesus and Greece – *Galatians, 1 and 2 Corinthians, Romans, 1 Timothy and Titus* written on the way.
- 59–63 Imprisonment in Caesarea and Rome (Acts 24–28) – *Ephesians, Philippians, Colossians, Philemon* and *2 Timothy* written from imprisonment.

hoped to visit on his way to Spain as he fulfilled his calling of spreading his gospel through the Gentile world. He had not been responsible for founding the Roman church (as he had many of the other churches to which he writes), and so does not assume the same authority in relation to them as he does over others. Equally, he has not had reason to be kept in detailed touch with what was wrong there, so has little reason to be upbraiding them.

His gospel is summed up in two sentences which follow his opening greeting: 'it is God's power to save all who believe, first the Jews and also the Gentiles. For the gospel reveals how God puts man right with himself' (1.16–17). This gospel is then elaborated in an exposure of man's wilful commitment to wrongdoing, which even the Jews' law cannot undo (1.18–3.20). On the contrary, it is only undone by God himself. By sending Christ to die for us he makes it possible for us to be put right with him and to start a new life, freed from the domination by wrongdoing that characterized us before (3.21–8.39). Lest this should seem to compromise the position of the Jews, Paul expounds how God is still committed to them (9.1–11.36). Then he reminds his readers how Christians are called to respond to God's love by committing themselves to him, a commitment Paul itemizes in various ways (12.1–15.13) before closing with further details of his personal plans, and lengthy greetings.

1 Corinthians is hardly any shorter than Romans, but quite different in atmosphere. Here was a church that Paul founded, and (as we have noted) one from which he has had correspondence and independent news. At point after point what he hears appals him. Whether he looks at their theology, their personal lives or their worship, he finds much cause for concern. It is all the more appalling since it is accompanied by what strikes Paul as a naïvely conceited estimate of their spiritual maturity. It is in the course of his dealing with these vagaries, however, that Paul puts on paper some of the paragraphs that we would have been most sorry not to have: his account of the origin of the Lord's supper (the Holy Communion or Eucharist), his 'hymn to love', and his exposition of the fact and the importance of Jesus's resurrection (chapters 11, 13 and 15).

Behind the problems raised by the Corinthian Christians are recurring dangers in the early church, fundamentally false attitudes that twist the whole nature of the faith. One is a very negative attitude to the body – the belief that the soul is all that really matters. If this is so, then it does not matter how a Christian behaves outwardly – his soul is not affected. On the contrary, Paul believes, Jesus came in the flesh, and what a man does with his body affects his whole person. The view Paul is confronting is one aspect of what came to be called 'Gnosticism' (see further under Colossians below).

Paul perceives fundamental questions underlying sometimes trivial outward questions, and his approach is not just to give simple authoritarian answers to the problems the Corinthians raise, but to take them to the heart of the issues that the questions involve, and to expound the fundamental Christian truths whose perspective needs to be applied to the situation: the message of the cross, the fact that God's Spirit lives in them, the calling to be concerned for my brother rather than for my rights, the importance of love, the fact of the resurrection.

2 *Corinthians* is called by that title because it is the later of the two letters to Corinth that appear in the Bible, but references in these letters indicate that there were others that have not survived, and this letter is actually at least the third or fourth Paul wrote to Corinth. Here we can see he is dealing with the same difficult congregation as before, but in a very different way. It is perhaps not surprising if they have reacted against the straight talking embodied in 1 Corinthians. The fact that Paul has not kept to his alleged plans to come to see them gives them the opportunity to accuse him of being weak-willed and inconsistent, good at writing angry letters but scared of eyeball-to-eyeball confrontation, claiming apostolic authority but lacking real apostolic credentials. This leads Paul to show a quite different side of himself. He describes how the real credential of an apostle is the mark of the cross, and this he bears. Although Paul has had his mystical experiences, the heart of his Christian experience is his bearing the cross of Christ: but in

this he finds not despair but hope, because there he finds the comfort of Christ, and there he proves that the time when he is weak is, paradoxically, when he is really strong.

The theme of the suffering involved in being a Christian recurs in *Philippians*, where Paul calmly weighs against each other the relative merits of staying alive or dying so as to be with Christ. Philippians is a letter full of rejoicing. The combination of suffering and joy reappears in *1 Peter*. (Fewer of the letters of James, Peter, Jude and John were included in the New Testament, so they are known by their author, rather than by their audience, as Paul's were: but many of them, like Paul's, were written to churches in particular areas.) It is also a dominant theme in Revelation, as we shall see in chapter 13, and we are reminded by its recurrence that to be a Christian minister, or just an ordinary Christian, in the early years of the church was often a dangerous affair. Christianity was regarded as a subversive movement. It was subversive of Judaism (because it suggested that the law was finished). It was subversive of the Roman empire (because it refused to give the emperor the homage that it believed belonged only to God). Thus Christians often had to pay for their beliefs.

Galatians introduces us to another of the underlying attitudes among some Christians which Paul saw as undermining the nature of the gospel. Many Christians of Jewish background believed that when a person came to believe in Jesus he had to begin keeping the Jewish law. If the Corinthians undervalued the importance of a man's outward life, the Galatians overestimated it. Thus Paul has to say to the Galatians the opposite to what he said to the Corinthians. Their relationship with Christ does not hang on keeping outward laws – they have been freed from all that.

Thus Galatians is dominated, to an even greater extent than Romans, by the question of how a man is put right with God (the technical term for this is 'justification'). Men everywhere seek to make a mark for themselves and to get people to accept and admire them by doing things. In practice, though, we never seem able to do enough to be sure of this status. Galatians and Romans declare that we can have this status anyway, because

God is willing to accept us without our achieving anything at all.

Paul's defence of his apostolic position in Galatians leads to his giving his own account of some of the key incidents in his life. He speaks of his devotion as a Jew, his ruthless opposition to the church of Christ, and of Jesus appearing to him and turning his life upside down. He goes into detail as to his relationship with the Christian mission based on Jerusalem – his original independence of them, their acceptance of him, and his willingness to stand up to them when they were wrong. The letter unveils some of the fierce confrontations that went on within the Christian movement from the beginning, especially over the key question of the place of Gentiles within a movement that was thoroughly Jewish in its origin and background.

Ephesians and *Colossians* overlap considerably in their themes, and include some of the most developed of Paul's theology, on who Christ is, on what he has achieved, and on what it means to be his people. In Colossians, in particular, Paul confronts beliefs present in other religions of his day, and shows how faith in Christ is different from and superior to them. Some of Paul's comments suggest that the Colossian Christians were being urged to accept Jewish practices such as circumcision, kosher laws and keeping the sabbath and festivals. But there were beliefs other than mainstream Jewish ones involved. The worship of angels (2.16), and the downgrading of Christ (whose supreme importance Paul therefore emphasizes, 1.15–20), suggests the belief in a varied hierarchy of supernatural figures between man and God. At about this time the religion called Gnosticism was developing. Gnosticism means 'knowledge-ism' and suggests that we get to God in heaven by having the secret doctrines and 'passwords' which enable us to elude the hostile supernatural beings between us and God. Gnostics understood Jesus within this framework: Paul believes this is fundamentally mistaken. Jesus is too big for it, and the gospel is not an esoteric secret but a divinely revealed public message.

The letters to the *Thessalonians* are distinctive for their dealing with questions to do with the end of history and the end of the individual's life. People are not to be so intent on Christ's coming back that they give up work! Nor are they to be so overcome by grief when someone dies that they look as if they have no special reason for hope. 1 Thessalonians is generally accepted as the earliest of Paul's letters in the New Testament, and its clearly formulated picture of the events to take place when Christ comes again is striking. But the hope of Christ's return is a central concern also of later letters such as 2 *Peter* and *Jude*. Both of these emphasize that this event will be a moment of judgement on false belief, and 2 Peter especially warns lest anyone becomes slack in his Christian profession because the coming of Christ seems to be delayed.

Hebrews is more like a sermon than a letter (though it ends with one or two greetings). It challenges its readers to take their Christian calling more seriously and to see that the church is called to a life of steadfast pilgrimage. They are to persevere and not to waver.

The title 'Hebrews' reflects the Jewish concern of the letter. Its theme is the superiority of Christ over the various features of the Jewish religion. These were all right in their way – Moses, the revelation on Mount Sinai, the tabernacle and its sacrifices – but at every point Christ fulfils the same function as they did, but goes far beyond what they could achieve. The way the writer argues his points (who he was, we do not know) is by taking sections of the Old Testament that discuss the themes he wants to take up, and preaching a Christian sermonette on this text.

James is another sermon-like letter, and another Jewish document, though in a different sense. There is very little that is explicitly Christian in it; if we omitted the actual references to Christ in 2.1 and 3.1., it could be a Jewish sermon. Its concern is the opposite of Galatians. Whereas the Galatian Christians were inclined to over-emphasize Christian obedience, James's audience apparently take it too lightly. Paul in Galatians (and Romans) says, 'You are right with God not because you live in obedience to him, but just because of trusting in Christ' (and adds, 'You only have to look at Abraham for an illustration of that'). James has to say the opposite: 'You are not right with

God just because of trusting in Christ: you have to live in obedience to him' (and James, too, adds, 'You only have to look at Abraham for an illustration of that'). The two emphases are designed to confront two different mistakes. So James concentrates on getting his readers to live lives worthy of the faith they profess.

1 and 2 John have the same atmosphere as John's gospel. There are many references to 'light' and 'life' and 'love'. But whereas the gospel was written so that people might believe and have life (John 20.31), the letters were written so that people might *know* that they have life (1 John 5.13) – in other words, so that they would be sure of their position as Christians. John points his readers to the tests they can make of their own lives in order to see whether they do really belong to Christ.

Finally, the letters to *Timothy, Titus* and *Philemon,* and *3 John,* are more personal. Philemon is the only really private letter, appealing for clemency to a runaway slave. Yet even this letter is part of the ministry of Paul as an apostle concerned with the relationship between his spiritual brother Philemon and his spiritual son Onesimus. The other three are written to leaders of churches, about how to fulfil their ministry. They emphasize the importance of establishing a stable ministry in the church, of seeing that the church holds on firmly to the scriptures (the Old Testament) and to the truth of Christ, and of guarding against false beliefs.

13

The visions of the seers:

Daniel, Revelation

Daniel can be described as a prophet (Matthew 24.15) and the book of Daniel begins with stories like some that come in other parts of the Old Testament, as we have seen in chapter 7. Revelation refers to itself as a prophecy (1.3), and it begins and ends like a letter. Nevertheless the book of Daniel and the Revelation to John are so different from the works of the prophets (or the other parts of both Old and New Testaments) that they deserve to be looked at separately. And the aspects in which they are distinctive are just those in which they have many points of contact with each other.

These distinguishing features are of two kinds. One is the way in which the two writers express themselves. Their teaching comes predominantly in the form of the report of visions, and they thus make a very clear claim to have received their teaching direct from God. Prophets and apostles also tell of their visions (e.g. Zechariah; Paul in 2 Corinthians 12), though these experiences are not as prominent as they are in Daniel and Revelation. Indeed, many Christians since biblical times, and many non-Christians, have claimed to have had visions, and there is no reason to say that all of these must have been the product of over-fertile imaginations. Nowadays, scientists are less inclined to be dismissive of psychic or extra-sensory phenomena than was once the case, and particular examples need to be looked at on their merits.

Hardly anything in these visions is expressed in a straightforward way. History after Daniel's time is related in code and symbol: Revelation describes heaven with its thrones, with the lamb in the centre, with its temple, altar, and worshippers;

calamity to come is described in terms of animals arising from the sea and bowls pouring out plagues. Frequently it is difficult to know where literal description ends and where symbolism begins, and to see what the symbols mean. The difficulty of understanding what Revelation means by the beast or the thousand-year reign of Christ has led to the formulation of many different theories as to their right interpretation.

The second type of distinctive feature one finds in Daniel and Revelation is in their actual beliefs and teaching. To begin with, they each have a bleak view of the world and of history. As we have seen, the prophets assume that God is at work within history and that he fulfils his purpose by means of the decisions made by kings and nations. Either God's people were obedient to God and doing well, or they were disobedient and in trouble. But in the periods to which the book of Daniel and Revelation refer, history did not seem to be working out in this way. Daniel speaks of the Maccabaean period (second century BC), when the Jewish people had committed no gross sin, but were oppressed by the Seleucid King Antiochus, who even prevented proper worship of Yahweh. Revelation addresses itself to the predicament of Christians pressured and persecuted by the Roman empire in the later part of the first century AD. In both periods, history seemed to be working against God's purpose, and thus the two authors see this world as dominated by powers of evil. They believe God is ultimately in control, but that at the moment he is letting evil have its way. They assume, however, that the days of evil are numbered, and that a day will come when God vindicates his people and establishes his kingdom.

A consequence of this view is that Daniel and Revelation do not have the same challenge to moral living that characterizes the prophets. The prophets believe that there is a link between how men behave and how history works out. Daniel and Revelation cannot see that this is the case in their day, and therefore they do not demand repentance and commitment to God's moral will with the urgency that appears in the prophets. On the other hand, they do deliver a strong challenge regarding personal faithfulness to God despite the pressures that a crisis brings upon people. Daniel makes this point by its stories, Revelation by its promises to 'those who win the victory'.

In Daniel and Revelation, the supernatural world is more clearly characterized, than in other parts of the Bible. As well as references to evil powers, there are many allusions to angels and spirits. It may be that this in part reflects increased awareness of the greatness of God. If God is so absolutely on high, then there is increasing interest in beings such as angels through whom he acts in the world.

To what did the visions in Daniel and Revelation refer? Broadly, two main views may be described. One is that the seer is describing events that are to follow centuries (even millennia) after his time, leading up to the end of the world. According to this theory, Daniel is living in the exile but declaring what is to happen over the following centuries up to the Maccabees, and looking beyond that to the coming of Christ and his second coming. Revelation is describing in outline the epochs of history that are to follow from the coming of Christ to his second coming and the end of the world.

The second view is that the authors are men with a message for their own day. Thus the author of Daniel is actually living in the Maccabaean period; describing history from the exile onwards as if he were predicting the future, is simply a dramatic device. He is thus assuring his contemporaries that God really is in control of their destinies, by suggesting that it has all been working out in a way controlled by God. Similarly, in the book of Revelation, John is throughout describing not calamities of the distant future but the crisis of the present; and he is declaring that God is in control and is bringing the consummation of his purpose.

The ambiguity of the visions and their symbolism is such that it is difficult to prove whether either of these approaches is right. I personally think the second makes more sense, and is more of a piece with the way other parts of the Bible speak, but in what follows I will try to avoid prejudging this question as far as possible.

DANIEL

The visions in the book of Daniel begin with the period of the exile, in the time of Daniel himself, when Nebuchadnezzar and the Babylonians controlled the Jews' destiny. They go on to the Maccabaean period, when Antiochus Epiphanes and the Seleucids ruled Palestine (see chapter 2 above).

Nebuchadnezzar the Babylonian, along with Cyrus the Persian, and other sixth century figures, are explicitly mentioned in connection with the visions. Antiochus is not actually named, but his actions are particularly clearly referred to in the last vision (chapter 11–12). This gives a detailed summary of the history of the Greek period up to Antiochus's attempt to put an end to the Jews' worship of their God, though it does not actually name any of the figures. Instead they are simply referred to as 'the king of Syria', 'the king of Egypt', and so on. The vision then promises that God will intervene in this 'time of trouble', and bring judgement and resurrection. Three and a half years (seven is a symbolic perfect number, and the figure represents half of this) will elapse before this deliverance: in other words, the period of oppression is limited and within God's control.

The same kind of reckoning appears in the previous vision (chapter 9), which follows a prayer of confession on Daniel's part on behalf of his people. The temple sacrifices are to be suspended by an invading king for three and a half years at the end of a period of seventy times seven years (approximately the time from the exile to the Maccabees). But then the invader will be dealt with.

This crisis in Jerusalem caused by Antiochus is described by the vision in chapter 8, where the protagonists are identified as the various horns of a ram. Here the period of oppression is 1,150 days – again, a period of rather more than three years. But this vision, too, promises that the affliction will be supernaturally ended.

The first two visions in the book (chapters 2 and 7) are similar to each other. In symbols they describe four successive empires, beginning with the Babylonians. They concentrate on the fourth empire, however, which (to judge from the parallels

A KEY TO THE VISIONS IN DANIEL

	chapter 2	chapter 7	chapter 8	chapter 9	chapters 10–12
Babylonians	gold	lion/ eagle	—	7 times 7 years	—
Medes and Persians	silver then bronze	bear then leopard	ram with two horns	┬	five kings
Greeks (a) Alexander's empire	iron	horned beast	goat with prominent horn	7 times 62 years	mighty king of Greece
(b) empire divided	iron and clay feet	ten horns	four horns	┴	breaking of his kingdom
(c) Antiochus		little horn	little horn	3½ years of horror	battles between kings of Egypt and Syria
God's act (a) destruction	stone strikes iron and clay feet	beast killed	last king destroyed	horror ends	King of Syria dies
(b) new act	stone becomes mountain	empire given to human figure			Israelites saved, dead rise

with the other visions) is apparently again that ruled by Antiochus. Once more this empire is marvellously ended after three and a half years (7.25). Distinctive to one of these visions is the figure like a human being (7.13) to whom sovereignty is given after the fourth empire's fall. This figure represents the people of God (7.27). The symbol became important in later Jewish writings, and it is taken up as a title for Jesus himself (see, for instance, Mark 2.28; in the New Testament it is translated by the more usual but more cryptic phrase 'Son of Man').

The details of Daniel's visions are strange and puzzling, but the main drift is clear. Each speaks to the people of God in the terrible crisis that the oppression of Antiochus brought. They declare that the events of history, including such a crisis, are in God's control. These events are foreseen by him; they do not surprise him. He knows how long he is going to let the crisis last, and how he is going to bring it to an end.

And the Jews did see Antiochus off.

REVELATION

The book begins with letters to seven churches in the province of Asia (modern Turkey), challenging them about their faithfulness and promising God's own faithfulness to those who are really committed to him. Then the visions proper begin. First they describe a scene in heaven, where God is enthroned, surrounded by his heavenly worshippers. He holds a scroll with seven seals; it contains an outline of history which is under his control. But who can be allowed to open the scroll? A 'Lamb standing in the centre of the throne' – a lamb which 'appeared to have been killed' (Jesus Christ) – is declared worthy to do so, and thus the unveiling can begin. Ironically, it seems to conceal at the same time as it reveals, for although one can describe the contents, it is much more difficult to be sure what the author meant by them.

The scroll tells of seven calamities which befall the earth (chapters 4–7). The first of these, such as war, are caused by men, but the later ones are 'natural' disasters such as earthquakes. The sequence is relieved only by the picture of a vast multitude which is protected from the calamities by the Lamb.

The seventh seal unfolds a second sequence of seven 'natural' disasters, heralded by means of trumpets blown by angels (chapters 8–11). This sequence ends with the power to rule over the world belonging to our Lord and his Messiah.

The most bizarre of the visions now follows (chapters 12–14), with extraordinary scenes describing a dragon which seeks to devour a new-born child, and grotesque beasts arising from earth and sea. On behalf of the dragon (which explicitly symbolizes the Devil), the beasts compete with God for the allegiance of men. The Lamb and his 144,000 followers stand, however, and the visions promise that God will judge the powers of evil and their followers. The features of the visions here are very reminiscent of those in Daniel, though the detail is more developed.

The story is not over, however. The visions now describe seven plagues, 'the final expression of God's wrath', further 'natural' calamities bringing God's judgement on the beast (chapter 15). After these plagues, we read a description of the downfall of 'the great prostitute', Babylon, which represents Rome, 'the great city that rules over the kings of the earth' (17.18). God's people are challenged not to defile themselves by being involved with her. As a further encouragement to that end, Revelation closes with much more attractive pictures of the Lamb's marriage feast, the death of the beast, the defeat of Satan, the new heaven and earth, the new Jerusalem, and the promise that Jesus is coming again (chapters 21–22).

In my opinion, two principles are worth bearing in mind as we read through this strange book. The first is that Revelation had a message for its own day. The book declares that the oppressive and persecuting Roman empire (and the other persecutors of the church) will not have the last word; God will. Many of the features need to be understood against the background of the Roman empire.

And yet the Roman empire becomes a symbol of something much bigger: it is the very embodiment of the powers of evil asserted against the purpose of God and the people of God. The significance of the book thus points beyond one particular historical situation, because it promises that God is the Lord who deals with any such self-assertive power. History is in God's control. The slain Lamb holds the world's destiny. And thus finally the book points us to the day when God will finally bring his 'new Jerusalem', a vision for the future which is offered as an inspiration to those who worship God and the Lamb, to encourage them to remain faithful despite suffering in the present.

The vision of a thousand-year reign of Christ, which comes towards the end of the book but just before these final chapters (chapter 20), has been regarded as of great significance as a portrayal of the 'millennium', usually regarded as an age of great blessing still to come and preceding the final consummation of God's purpose. This chapter is the Bible's only reference to such a millennium, and the characteristic ambiguity of Revelation's symbolism has led to wide disagreement as to what the millennium means. It is probably unwise to base too much on this chapter because we cannot be sure how the picture given there is meant to relate to other pictures in the book.

Israel's response to God

There is a sense in which the whole Bible is the Jews' response to what God has done and how he has spoken. But there are some parts in which this response is overtly expressed. The book of Psalms contains psalms of praise and thanksgiving as the writer contemplates God's character and actions. There are also the psalms of prayer (and Lamentations) which are Israel's response to God when he seems to allow calamity to befall her.

In two other Old Testament books, however, Ecclesiastes and Job, it is not the voice of faith, but the voice of doubt which is dominant, and the Bible includes in its library that genuinely human voice; it accepts the possibility of questioning God.

14

Prayer and praise:

Psalms, Lamentations

Before we look at the various types of psalms, we may note some of the things they have in common. First, they are, of course, poetry. They are not like our hymns in having regular numbers of words in a line, with some lines rhyming, and so on. Most verses have two lines, and these lines complement each other in some way. They may say similar things twice in different words:

> Sinners will be condemned by God
> And kept apart from God's own people. (1.5)

Or they may make two converse statements:

> The righteous are guided and protected by the Lord
> But the evil are on the way to their doom. (1.6)

Or the second line may simply complete the first, taking its thought further:

> I call to the Lord for help
> And from his sacred hill he answers me. (2.4)

But in one way or another, the verse is thus usually the unit of thought.

Within each line, there is often a regular number of words. Now this is not obvious in English, because Hebrew uses many compound words (words strung together to make one longer word). But in Hebrew there are most often three words in each line:

Come, let-us-praise the-Lord!
Let-us-sing-for-joy to-God, who-protects-us!
Let-us-come before-him with-thanksgiving . . . (95.1–2)

In more prayerful psalms, there are often three words in the first line and only two in the second – this gives more of a limping lilt to the poetry:

Listen-to my-words, O Lord,
And-hear my-sighs.
Listen-to my-cry for-help,
My-God and-king. (5.1–2)

(To be honest, the verses do not consistently work out as neatly as this!)

We do not know how the psalms were sung when they were first written. They are sung in the synagogue today by a method similar to plainsong, but it is impossible to tell whether this was the style used in the temple. I like to think it would rather have been a method that pays more attention to the way the poetry of the psalms works. The modern 'Gelineau' psalms are an attempt to devise such a method: the musical note changes when you move from one compound Hebrew word to the next. The musical interest is thus spread through the line rather than being confined to the end of the line as it is in plainsong and Anglican chanting. If the Israelites did not sing the psalms by a Gelineau-type method, they ought to have done!

The psalms begin with titles, which GNB puts in the margin, probably in part because we do not understand many of them. Many are notes indicating where the psalm came from: 'a poem by the sons of Korah' (e.g. 44) was one in the hymnbook of the Korahites, and so on. Others give directions for the use of the psalm or for its musical accompaniment. Several refer to incidents in David's life.

Most do not indicate when they were written, however. We may make guesses as to the historical circumstances which produced a particular psalm, but these are only guesses. We can be more certain, at least in a general sense, of the circumstances in which the psalms were actually used once they had been written. The book of Psalms is Israel's hymnbook and prayerbook; a hymnbook and prayerbook is most at home in church, and the book of Psalms is the hymnbook of the temple.

The temple was the centre of religious faith for the Israelite to a greater extent than a church building is for a Christian. Within Christianity, indeed, buildings of brick and stone cease to have any great significance. God's Holy Spirit came to dwell among Christians themselves. As Jesus put it, he himself is present wherever a few people gather in his name. This happens without them having to be in a special building.

To Israel, however, God had promised that they would know his presence in the temple. This is often expressed in terms of his 'name' being there. The Israelites knew that God himself in his totality could not be in the temple – the whole heaven was not large enough to hold him, so how could a man-made building (1 Kings 8.27)? But Israel knew God's name. Now in Israel a name characteristically revealed something about a person: it expressed his parents' hopes for him, or his own character or destiny. 'Adam' was made of earth (Hebrew '*adamah*': see Genesis 2.7), 'Abraham' suggested the phrase 'father of many nations' (see Genesis 17.5), Solomon's reign was characterized by peace and prosperity ('*shalom*', see 1 Chronicles 22.9).

The distinctive name of the God of Israel was Yahweh. It does not mean 'Lord', as GNB translates it (see the GNB Preface). It is God's personal name, revealed to Israel. And this name, too, has a meaning: 'Yahweh' suggests the one who is there, the one who makes his presence felt (see chapter 4).

So Israel knew God's name; she therefore knew something of his character. When she uttered his name she knew something of his presence: thus, because the temple was the place where Yahweh's name was declared in worship, the temple was the place where his presence was known.

The temple was thus the centre of the religious life of Israel. Nation and individuals came here at moments of joy and in times of crisis (as Samuel, Kings, and Chronicles show) to bring their praise and their prayer. And the book of Psalms is a collection of these praises and prayers.

As is the case with the messages of the prophets, the psalms have various types of outward shape and form, and it is worthwhile trying to see what different types of psalm have in common, and how the types differ from each other. Comparing examples of the same type both helps to understand what all these examples meant to Israel, and enables us to appreciate what may be their individually distinctive features.

The different types in fact illustrate different ways of speaking to God. The kind of basic exclamations human beings make to one another – 'please', 'help', 'sorry', 'thank you', 'that's great', 'you're great', 'I love you' – these are the fundamental things man finds himself saying to God, too.

'PLEASE', 'HELP', 'SORRY'

Often the psalms express man's need. Some of these are the prayers of the whole people, apparently gathered in the temple in some national crisis. Psalm 74, for instance, describes the devastation wrought by enemies and pleads with God to do something about it. Psalm 60 similarly speaks of the land falling apart because God has let the nation be defeated. Towards the end of this psalm, however, an 'I' speaks – 'Who, O God, will take me into the fortified city? Who will lead me to Edom?' Presumably here the king, as Israel's leader in battle, speaks. The king would be prominent in the people's worship, especially on an occasion of national crisis or national rejoicing.

It makes sense to see many other psalms which only speak of 'I' as similarly uttered by the king, or uttered on his behalf, on such occasions. Such psalms as 3, 5, and 25, then, exemplify the prayer of the nation's leader when the nation is under pressure.

Other 'I' psalms show less indication that they must be the prayers of the king, and these are more likely to have been written for the use of private individuals. They may be the lament of someone oppressed by the wicked, or a sick man's prayer for healing, or a sinner's plea for forgiveness: indeed these motifs may be interwoven (e.g. Psalms 38, 39, 41).

Presumably in such situations an individual would come (perhaps with his family and friends) to the temple to pray, and these are the psalms he would use. Other 'I' psalms, again, may be intended for the whole congregation to use. A clear example outside the Psalms is Lamentations 3, a prayer like the others in Lamentations which was written for the people to use after the destruction of Jerusalem, but one which speaks of 'I'.

Although these prayers came out of diverse background situations, there are certain elements in them which tend to recur.

1) *This is how I feel.* After an introduction which calls on God and which may introduce the psalmist's prayer, the feature which dominates these prayers (in the sense that it occupies most verses in the psalm) is the description of the psalmist's need, in the form of a lament at the suffering or oppression he is undergoing. He describes his affliction at some length, no doubt in part as a way of getting it off his chest to God (who is the one who can do something about it). The experience of affliction may be described from three perspectives: the psalmist speaks of 'they', 'I', and 'you'. He thus speaks of the undeserved hostility and deceit which *other people* have shown to him; of the loneliness and oppression which *he himself* feels; and, worst of all, of how *God* has let him down and abandoned him. The descriptions are often moving.

2) *This is why you should respond to my prayer.* The psalmists commonly go on from their lament to say that, nevertheless, they do trust God to respond to them in their need. They still believe that he alone can save them. We have spoken of this as a reason why God should answer their prayer, but in these declarations of praise to God and trust in him, we can also hear them reassuring themselves and seeking to build up the trust which actual present experience seems to belie.

As well as confessing their trust in God, they sometimes also confess their sin against God: their acknowledgement of sin clears the way to God's forgiveness and restoration. At least as often, however, they protest that they have *not* acted wrongly, that it cannot be said that the misfortune which has come upon them is all that they deserve. They have been faithful to God; the trouble is, he has not been faithful to them. So again, they urge God to respond by denying that their sin is a reason why he should not be faithful. (Clearly the claim not to have sinned could be arrogant – and is arrogant, if they are implying that they have never done anything wrong. But they are rather saying that they have not gone back on their commitment to God in such a way as to deserve the kind of affliction they are experiencing.)

3) *So this is what I ask for.* The psalmist's actual prayer is a relatively short section in the psalm as a whole. Indeed, even the prayer part is not very specific – there is no list of precise requests which the psalmist brings. It might be summed up in a phrase such as 'Save me', or even simply 'Do something'. But often the aspects of affliction described earlier are picked up in the actual prayer. With respect to God, the psalmist prays that he may turn in love to his servant, instead of seeming to have his face turned away; and that he may intervene in the situation, instead of seeming to do nothing. With respect to his enemies, he may pray that they may be confuted and that judgement may come on them in turn. With respect to himself, he prays for healing, victory, restoration.

4) *God will answer me!* Often in the psalms there is a change of mood before the end: the psalmist begins to speak as if his prayer has been answered (see, for example, the transition in Psalm 28 between verses 5 and 6). It may be that this simply expresses his belief that the Lord does hear prayer and therefore that his burden has been passed over to the Lord (another possibility is that the final verses of the psalm were sung when the psalmist returned to the temple to praise God after he had experienced the answer to his prayer). But on some occasions, at least, at this point in the psalm the supplicant was verbally assured by a priest or prophet that the Lord had heard and would respond (see the message incorporated into Psalm 12 – verse 5 – and into Psalm 60 – verses 6–8). It is to this that he responds in praise as the mood of the psalm changes.

The note of praise appears frequently even in these prayers in need. It commonly closes the psalm. As the psalmist looks forward to the Lord answering his prayer, he looks in anticipatory praise even beyond that to the privilege, responsibility, and joy of returning to the temple, as we have noted above, to give public acknowledgement of the grace and power of the God who has responded to him.

LAMENTATIONS

The five poems which make up Lamentations are simply examples of the prayers we have been looking at, examples which derive from one particular disaster, the destruction of Jerusalem in 587 BC. In describing *how I feel,* they give us a moving description of the sufferings and sorrows of the experience: the desolation of the city which God had said he would protect and where he had lived in the temple, the gloating of Israel's enemies, the degradation of the people (women eating their own children), the abandonment and anger of God himself. The five poems each have twenty-two units, twenty-two being the number of letters in the Hebrew alphabet, and in chapters 1–4 each unit begins with a different letter of the alphabet: they are, as it were, expressions of grief from A to Z.

So why should God respond to their prayer? Lamentations acknowledges that the affliction was entirely deserved. The people had been unfaithful to God, and here they confess that the punishment which has come upon them is deserved. They have no claims on God. If he answers (and Lamentations acknowledges it is a big 'if'), it will be because of his mercy, not their rights. Their only hope is his 'unfailing love and mercy' (3.22).

What they ask for is for a time when God, in this unfailing love, 'looks down from heaven and sees us' (3.50). 'Bring us back to you, Lord! Bring us back! Restore our ancient glory' (5.21). Combined with this plea is a recurrent appeal to God, in all justice, to punish their attackers as he has punished them.

The conviction that *God will answer me* is not as confidently expressed as it is in the psalms. Lamentations still believes God does answer (see 3.55–60). But the poems end with a question rather than a statement, 'Or have you rejected us for ever?' (5.22). The people deserve no more, they know, and too fervent a conviction beyond that would surely belie their confession of sin.

'THANK YOU', 'THAT'S GREAT', 'YOU'RE GREAT', 'I LOVE YOU'

Thank you. The prayers look forward to thanksgiving and praise; so it is appropriate next to look at those psalms which express thanksgiving for God's response to prayer. These belong to the temple, of course; but the feelings they express do not have their origin in the temple. The psalm itself is but the formalizing of a response made at the moment of Yahweh's act – we can sometimes trace this response in the Old Testament's narratives of the events themselves. When God answered Israel's prayer by taking them through the Red Sea and enabling them to escape from their pursuers, 'the prophet Miriam, Aaron's sister, took her tambourine, and all the women followed her, playing tambourines and dancing. Miriam sang for them: "Sing to the Lord, because he has won a glorious victory, he has thrown the horses and their riders into the sea" ' (Exodus 15.20–21).

Praise begins in life. But then the person who has had his prayer answered comes before the Lord and the Lord's people to say so. Merely giving thanks in private would not be enough – the Lord deserves public acknowledgement for what he has done, and the psalmist is glad to offer it. He had promised in his lament that he would come back to praise God for answering his prayer, and now he does so.

The thanksgiving itself is essentially a grateful look back, with several natural elements. The psalmist recalls the predicament he had been in – physical and emotional distress, the threat of death itself, and the feeling of the absence and neglect of God himself. He recalls the urgent plea he made to God in this situation. With joy he recalls how God did exactly as he asked. God, whose face had seemed hidden and uncaring, turned to him; then he acted to restore the psalmist to physical and emotional well-being and to the joy and praise which are supposed to characterize the believer's life. But as the prayers talk not so much about what I think God should do, as about what are the facts I think he should do something about, so the thanksgivings talk not so much about what are the grateful feelings of the psalmist, but what are the facts he feels grateful about.

This praise the psalmist promises he will continue to offer, not merely for God's responses to particular prayers, but for all that God has done and is for his people, all that of which his recent experience of God's grace has given the psalmist a fresh conviction.

That's great. As the prayers lead logically to the thanksgivings, the thanksgivings lead logically to the psalms of praise. The difference is that the psalms of praise do not have a particular recent experience to rejoice in; they have more permanent things in mind.

Sometimes this praise is indirect: God is praised by glorying in what belongs to him, what he has made, what he gives. One theme which comes over particularly prominently in the psalms is God's activity as Lord of creation. God's sovereignty as creator lies behind both his sovereignty in history (on which 'the story of God and his people' concentrates, except in the opening chapters of Genesis) and his sovereignty in my personal experience (of which the prayers and thanksgivings speak).

Creation, as the psalms rejoice in it, is not merely the long-ago past event which set the world going. It is the present activity of God. He ensures that the powers of chaos cannot reassert themselves; the world is secure. He makes the rain fall and the grass grow: he thus feeds man and beast. The cosmos declares his glory.

Psalm 19, one that does rejoice in God's creation, goes on to add a note of praise to God for his word, and we have noted in chapter 9 that a lyrical joy in God's word appears in several psalms, most systematically in Psalm 119.

The psalms also rejoice in Jerusalem and its temple; we have looked already at something of the significance of this. Other peoples had their sacred city, their sacred hill, their sacred building. But the psalms are convinced that Jerusalem is the true centre of the world, because it is the city Yahweh chose; Mount Zion is the real mountain of God, despite its physical insignificance. The temple there is the true dwelling-place of the Lord Almighty.

So God is praised not only directly, by acknowledging him,

but by saying 'that's great' with regard to the world he creates, the word he utters, and the city he inhabits. As long as none of these comes to be rejoiced in independently of him, all is well.

You're great. There are further psalms which rejoice in God himself, which describe his character and his deeds, and make that a reason for praising him. They begin by calling people to praise: the whole world should be involved for this praise to be worthy of him, but often the psalmist is satisfied to call on all Israel. This invitation or challenge is then backed up by the reasons for it, which arise out of God's character. These reasons may be summed up in short phrases (like the verses of praise which close prayers). They may then be amplified by some rejoicing in how God has revealed himself in his characteristic areas of activity: in creation, in the great historical events such as the exodus which established Israel as a nation, and in the providence he exercises in the everyday lives of men and in the situations which confront his people.

CREEDS, BLESSINGS, PROMISES, CHALLENGES

The psalms are dominated by prayer and praise. But they have some other aspects which ought at least to be mentioned.

They begin with a blessing (Psalm 1) which describes the protection and prosperity God gives those who are committed to him. This is not the only psalm that brings a challenge: Psalms 15 and 24, for instance, remind the worshipper of the moral qualities that must characterize those who come into God's presence. Psalms 50 and 82 go beyond that in declaring God's judgement upon injustice. Nor is Psalm 1 the only one that declares the psalmist's own creed: 37, for instance, speaks of his conviction with regard to God's faithfulness, while 49 proclaims his belief that God will even rescue him from death.

After the blessing comes a promise concerning the king (Psalm 2), and here a major theme of the psalms is introduced. We have noted above that the 'I' of the psalms often seems to be the king. Here the psalms' concern with the king is explicit. God promises his commitment to him, because he is the means of God's lordship being exercised in the world. There are several psalms that speak of varied aspects of the king's significance: Psalm 72 prays for his fulfilment of the role of bringing justice; 89 recalls the promise made to David and asks for its fulfilment now; 45 prays for blessing on his marriage; and so on. These psalms for the king came to be interpreted messianically – that is, they came to express the hope that one day Israel would be given a king who would really live up to the theology of kingship expressed here – and they thus come to be applied to Jesus in the New Testament. But they were written with real present kings of David's line in Jerusalem in mind. They challenge them to live up to the kingly ideal and promise them God's commitment to them as they seek to do so.

15

Doubts and certainties:

Ecclesiastes, Job

It is slightly arbitrary to treat Ecclesiastes and Job in a different chapter from Proverbs, because these two books, too, embody the approach to life of Israel's wise men, and they, too, are meant to teach – in this sense they belong to 'The word of God to his people'. But they are books that speak to God as much as about God, yet with a very different accent from the one which praises God in the psalms. Yet even the psalms are often lamenting God's absence; and Ecclesiastes may be seen as taking to greater length the questioning of the point of it all which appears, for instance, in Psalms 49 and 73. Job, in turn, has many features which suggest an extended psalm of lament.

ECCLESIASTES

Ecclesiastes has been described as the most modern book in the Bible. It takes up many of the concerns of contemporary western society – freedom, justice, pleasure, success, progress, money, knowledge, ambition, power, sex – and asks what they are really worth, and whether they can make life worth while. The answer is a clear no; this is plain as the book begins, for it announces its theme in its opening lines: 'It is useless, useless, said the philosopher. Life is useless, all useless.' 'Useless' is a key word in the book. It means 'a breath' – something that has no body to it, a mere puff of wind.

The fundamental reason why life is useless is that death hangs over it: death, which despite all man's efforts he cannot avoid; death which is so unfair, cutting off in their prime people who ought to live long and happy lives (and ignoring people whose wrongdoing makes them deserve to die); death which is unpredictable, so that a man can never know when his day will come, and thus plan for it; death which is above all unpleasant. Not that Ecclesiastes (or, generally, other parts of the Old Testament) saw in death the flames of hell causing perpetual torment. Death just meant an end to all the good things: your body was stuck in a cold rock tomb to rot, and your personality joined the other pathetic personalities in Sheol, the home of the dead. It was a place characterized by what you couldn't do: there, Ecclesiastes says, there is no doing, no feeling, no thought, no knowledge, no wisdom, no reward, no acknowledgement, and no hope (9.5–6, 10). The most striking thing about death must be its boredom (and perhaps 'boring' is the twentieth century's most damning epithet!).

So what attitude are we to take to life? There are two attitudes that Ecclesiastes explicitly rejects. One is the indulgence in a frenzy of activity and achievement which hides from the truth of the human situation. That is just escapism. The other is the pie-in-the-sky solution that asserts, hopefully, that all will be put right after death. 'After all,' says Ecclesiastes, 'the same fate awaits man and animal alike. One dies just like the other. They are both going to the same place – the dust. How can anyone be sure that a man's spirit goes upwards while an animal's spirit goes down to the ground?' (3.19–21). (In the light of Jesus's resurrection, of course, the Christian has more to say about this.)

There is another possible response, which Ecclesiastes does not consider: would it not be logical to commit suicide? An intuition tells us not; but why not? I think Ecclesiastes' answer would be to point to the fact that we receive life as a gift from God, and it is not for us to spurn it or decide for ourselves when the spirit God gives is to be returned to him. And this fact, that it is God who gives life, is the fundamental conviction which forms Ecclesiastes' own attitude to life. We cannot understand the big questions, we cannot achieve the big things we would love to strive for. But the fact remains that we receive life from the creator himself, and although he remains an enigma, the personal everyday satisfactions of food and drink, work and personal relationships, and so on, may be received and enjoyed as his gifts. They are not to be treated as ultimate ends in themselves, nor devoured with the despair or abandon of 'Let us eat, drink, and be merry, for tomorrow we die', but received humbly, seriously, yet joyfully, as the things God *has* given; we must just accept the absence of what he has *not* given.

JOB

What is the book of Job about? The obvious answer is, it is about the problem of suffering; and it has a great deal to teach us about that topic. But why does it discuss the problem of suffering? The real concern of the book of Job is the question, 'What kind of relationship obtains between man and God?' It discusses the problem of suffering because Job's suffering makes Job into a test case with regard to this question.

We noted in chapter 11 that the wise men of Israel sought to instruct her in what attitudes to life worked. They believed that a righteous life was also a sensible life; God made life work in such a way that a moral life was also a happy and successful one. The belief may be true much of the time, but it is not always true; and what attitude do you take to the exceptions?

To let goodness be seen to be rewarded flaunts before us the temptation to be good for what we can get out of it: to turn the relationship between us and God into a commercial one. Commercial relationships have their place: business depends on people agreeing to give something in return for something else. In these relationships, our own interest, what we can get out of it, is uppermost in our mind. But we recognize that there is something more profound, more human, about the personal relationships in which people give to one another without thought for what they will get in return – when they keep on loving even when their love is spurned, when they demonstrate that 'love never gives up; its faith, hope and patience never fail' (1 Corinthians 13.7).

Which kind of relationship obtains between man and God? Job was a man who had proved that morality, conformity, and religion paid dividends (1.1–3). He was a model of piety and life. But was he only religious because it paid? This was 'the accuser's' explanation (1.8–10). ('Satan' is an ordinary Hebrew word for 'opponent' – it is not a proper name in the Old Testament, except perhaps 1 Chronicles 21, where there is no 'the' before the word.) Perhaps Job is only in it for what he can get out of it. And perhaps God himself only cultivates human adulation because he is lonely or it boosts his ego. Perhaps he is like the big boy who desperately needs to impress the little boys. Perhaps the whole relationship between God and man is a sham. It looks from the outside like one of love and trust, but

THE BOOK OF JOB

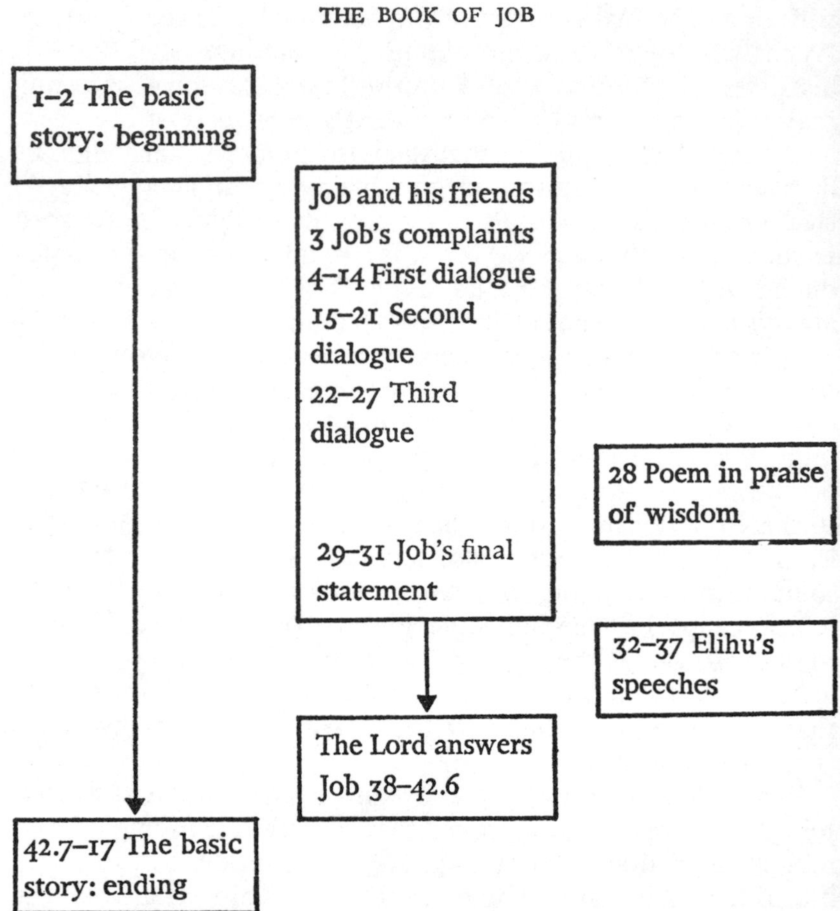

really it's only 'scratch my back and I'll scratch yours'. Not a personal relationship, but a commercial one.

How is it to be established whether God, or the accuser, is right? In a business relationship, if one party withdraws, the other party has the right to do so too. If you do not renew your subscription to the Automobile Association, the AAA service truck will not be available. If God withdraws his blessing from Job, will he still be uniquely blameless and upright, God-fearing and righteous?

The scenes that follow in Job's story show his life falling apart. He loses his possessions in a series of business calamities (1.14–17). He loses his sons and daughters in a natural disaster (1.18–19). He loses his health (2.7–8), his wife despairs (2.9), and his friends – who assume that the business relationship picture *is* the right one – conclude that he must have broken his side of the bargain, and berate him accordingly (chapters 4–27).

The drama opens up many questions other than the one from which the story starts. Job's own spiritual pilgrimage takes him along ways he could not have dreamed of before. His relationship with God undergoes the severest strains and his assertiveness has to be rebuked. But the Satan had predicted he would curse God, and his wife had urged him to do so. His friends had tried to browbeat him into confessing sins he had not committed. These things he did not do. And at the end of the story he is commended – he had spoken the truth (42.7) – and he is given new blessings. He never knew (as far as the story tells us) the reason for his experience. But the relationship was vindicated.

What insights on the problem of suffering are suggested by all this? In the course of this testing of the nature of the relationship between Job and God, the question of suffering is approached from various angles. Job's three friends assume, as we have seen, that Job suffers because of his sin. This assumption was one that came naturally to them: it was what 'the advice of the wise men' taught was the case. It was a truth that had proved itself over the generations; it was what orthodoxy had always taught, as Bildad especially emphasized. It was also the truth maintained by Eliphaz, though he adds an extra ground for accepting it: he has received a supernatural revelation concerning the matter (4.12–21).

And there is truth in this view. There is a connection between sin and suffering. This is true in a general sense – the amount of suffering in the world is at least in part to be explained as in various senses the result of human sin. And it is often true in detail with regard to particular situations (Paul, for instance, attributes certain illnesses and deaths among the Corinthians to their failure to 'recognize the meaning of the Lord's body' at the Lord's supper: 1 Corinthians 11.29–30). But Job receives a disproportionate share of the general suffering in the world; and he is not a notorious sinner. The theory does not cover him – unless the story of his life is first rewritten to include many sins (as it is, by the friends).

Elihu, the angry young man who appears towards the end of the debate (chapters 32–37), suggests a variation on this theme. Elihu is the great champion of human reason: he believes that God gave man his mind, and that man can find the answers if he will use his mind. Suffering, he declares, can be intended to bring us back to God. It is thus an expression of God's loving concern for his creatures. Again, this approach is one which is entirely biblical, but somehow not quite relevant: Job is a committed believer, so hardly in need of such chastening.

The author's own answer to the question, as we have seen, is that Job's suffering is sent as a test. And this view, too, can be paralleled elsewhere in the Bible (e.g. 1 Peter 1.7). But even the author's answer is irrelevant to the question, how was Job to cope with suffering: for Job was not told that this was the explanation. Job never gets an answer to his question, 'Why?', even though he could have been given one.

So what is Job's attitude? He is commended at the end of the story, because he had at least insisted on facing facts – unlike his friends, who rewrote the facts and made Job into a sinner in order that he could fit into their theories.

Nevertheless, he is not meekly accepting of what he has to go through. On the contrary, as he gets more and more annoyed with his friends, so he becomes more and more insistent that God is being unreasonable and more and more determined to clear his name. If necessary, he will be satisfied if this only comes about after death: envisaging this possibility, Job comes out with his famous 'I know that my redeemer liveth' (16.18–22; 19.23–27). But vindication and release after death are second best to the vindication he demands *now*!

Before Job's final review of his former happiness, present misery, and lifelong righteous conduct (chapters 29–31), there appears a poem about God's unfathomable wisdom (chapter 28). It offers a comment on the debate, which conveys an implicit judgement both on Job and on his friends. They think they have the truth all tied up; but they are wrong. Job sees that, and he wants to go beyond them – he thinks he is entitled to know the truth; but he is wrong, too. God's wisdom is unfathomable; the poem ends with the reminder which recurs through the wisdom books, that the humble worship of God provides the only starting point for beginning to understand his ways. The poem raises issues which will be taken further when God appears to Job.

When this happens, God in a sense thus grants Job the confrontation he has asked for. But Job finds the occasion is not one on which he is confronting God; it is God confronting him. It is God who asks the questions, not Job. The questions involve a conducted tour of the whole creation, in the course of which God keeps asking, 'Could you do that? Were you there when I made that? Can your mind understand that?' The purpose of the confrontation is to drive home a point which has in fact been made in the earlier speeches, though not with such force. God is the lord of creation, and it is impossible for man to question him or to aspire to understanding his purpose in its totality.

Job is prepared to grant the point (40.1–5). But when he does so, God does not stop questioning him. The confrontation resumes, and here centres on the question, what can Job do about the unfairness and injustice that often seems to characterize human life? Job complains about injustice, but he cannot himself do anything to lessen the element of unfairness in human experience. Having challenged him on this point, God now points to two strange creatures, Behemoth and Leviathan.

The point about these creatures is that, in the myths of the middle eastern peoples, they epitomized the power of evil and chaos asserted against goodness and order. But they are under God's control; they are, in fact, only animals (Israel's equivalent to the Loch Ness monster: theoretically fearsome, but in practice the object of fun). There are no powers of chaos and injustice, beyond God's control. The very creation shows that God's power and wisdom rule the world.

Job, however, had been questioning whether justice and providence were in control in the world – because in his own personal world they did not seem to be so. The person who suffers is challenged to believe, despite his suffering, that God's power and wisdom do rule. How his present experience fits into that, Job cannot see and God does not explain. But creation shows that God can be trusted, even where he cannot be understood.

The book, then, does accompany doubts with certainties. The Bible as a whole does not claim to answer every question: some questions have to be left to the mystery of God. But it does claim that, in the light of creation (and of the story of Israel and the story of the cross) there are enough certainties for us to carry on trusting even where we cannot understand.

The Bible today

In this book, we have been trying to understand the Bible for what it meant to those who wrote it, as we might investigate some other ancient book such as the writings of the Greeks, or the Koran, the holy book of the Moslems. In my Introduction, however, I noted that in order to appreciate the Bible, we had to take up a sympathetic approach to it. Whether or not we believe in God, we are trying to get inside the thinking of people who did believe in God. We are unlikely to gain any kind of real insight into their writings if we cannot suspend our beliefs and disbeliefs while we try to understand theirs. Actually, here again no more is required than is needed if I try to read the Koran. If as I read it, I am concerned only with proving it wrong, I will probably never understand it at all. I have to take as my aim the attempt to look at the world through its spectacles.

When I do that, however, I may well find that I let myself in for more than I bargained for. Unless the book I am trying to understand contains no sense at all, there are things I may learn from its insights. If I do manage to look at the world through its spectacles, I find that I am challenged to keep those spectacles on. In certain ways, at least, I find that they have the world in focus. I can hardly then throw them away and resume looking at the world the way I did before.

If this truth about the sensitive reading of an important book applies quite generally, it certainly applies to the Bible, which pushes us to an attitude of more than mere curiosity. It claims to provide definitive insights on the most urgent questions faced by men in every age: What is human life about? How is it that man's story is such a puzzling combination of achievement and failure, goodness and badness, success and degradation? Where is the world going? Is there a God, and (if so) what is he like, and on what basis can we relate to him? What sort of life ought we to live, and how can we live up even to the standards we do see?

The Bible's response to these questions, as we have seen, comes in the form of stories and statements. The statements tell us answers to some of the questions. The stories illustrate the answers and tell us how God did what needed to be done for these answers to work.

The story comes to a climax in Jesus Christ. In a mysterious way his death and resurrection made it possible for the relationship between man and God to be healed, and these events assure us that God is Lord of human history. Now we can enjoy that relationship which God intended for man from the beginning, and begin to live life in this world to the full, as God intended.

The New Testament, then, tells us the facts on which this life with God is based, and it tells us how it was worked out for the first Christian churches. Christians today cannot get away from the writings of the first Christians, those who were nearest to the Jesus of history himself. And if we want to follow in their footsteps, then we can learn from their experiences, their problems, their insights.

But we have to allow for the difference in situation between ourselves and the New Testament Christians. We belong to a different age and a different culture. We are not necessarily superior to them, although we are technologically more sophisticated. We, too, ask the perennial questions about life to which we referred above – the questions are largely timeless. But how we express the answer in the language of our day, and precisely how we work out their implications, will vary.

We have noted, for instance, that the New Testament Christians interpreted what Jesus's death means for the relationship between man and God, by picking up human experiences of their day and using them as illustrations of what happens between God and man. What God has done for us in Christ is like him paying the price for a slave's release from bondage (redemption), or like him offering a sacrifice in a temple to deal with divine displeasure (propitiation), or like him declaring a guilty man innocent because someone else has paid his penalty (justification), or like him mediating between two people who have been at enmity with each other (reconciliation). Now some of these pictures (probably the last two) can mean as much in our cultures today as they did in New Testament times. The first two, however, mean little, in western society at least. They need a lot of explanation before we can appreciate them. They also need to be supplemented by illustrations drawn from our everyday life, as Paul, for instance, drew them from his.

Again, the instructions that the New Testament gives are always related to the social conditions of the day. Usually this causes no problems: stealing or hypocrisy are as wrong in our culture as they were in the first century. But at some points, social customs do affect the validity of the instructions. The classic example is Paul's exhortation in 1 Corinthians 11, concerning the wearing of hats by Christian ladies. It is very possible that one reason Paul saw this as important is that in Corinth at the time, only women of loose morals appeared in public bare-headed. (We might compare the veiling accepted by Arab women today.) If this is right, then it is understandable that Paul does not want the Corinthian women, in parading their Christian freedom, to give the wrong impression. Today, however, putting on your best hat to go to church may have become almost a symbol of hypocrisy; so in obeying Paul to the letter we may miss the spirit of what he was saying, and in effect do the opposite of what he wanted.

On the other hand, we need to be wary of 'explaining away' the teaching of the Bible by saying it was all limited to its culture. More often than not, its teaching is applicable to our day in a straightforward way; the only question is whether we will accept it!

One further aspect of the challenge brought by the time-gap and culture-gap between the Bible and ourselves is the fact that often it does not address the precise problems with which we are concerned. It has lots to say about sexual morality – the only question, again, is whether we will accept it! It has nothing direct to say about conservation or genetic engineering (nothing direct, that is, though its understanding of God, man, and the world in a general sense will have implications for such questions). This means that the modern Christian cannot, like the Pharisee, say, 'I will make sure I do all that the Bible says, and then I shall know I have fulfilled God's will.' He has to do what the Bible says; but then also to ask what further theological and moral questions are raised by the world in which we now live and by the lives we have to live, and go on to ask, 'If that was how God spoke to his people in their situation in the Bible, what may he be saying to us now in ours?' And when someone says, 'This is what I believe God is calling us to do now,' he will test such a claim by asking, 'Is that the kind of thing that I would expect God to be saying, on the basis of what the Bible tells me he has already said and done?'

Christians have usually found that relating the New Testament to our day is not too complicated (perhaps it is in fact more complicated than they have thought!). On the other hand, they have found the Old Testament more difficult to handle, and so we will spend the final section of this book looking in particular at the meaning of the Old Testament for today.

We will do this by considering six ways in which a Christian may look at the Old Testament. There is value in each of them; different methods may be more illuminating when applied to different parts of the Old Testament.

I. THE OLD TESTAMENT IS THE BACKGROUND TO THE NEW TESTAMENT

We begin from the fact that the story of Jesus cannot be understood or accepted without taking the Old Testament into account, because the Old Testament was Jesus's Bible.

We have seen that one thing that struck people immediately about Jesus was the fact that he spoke 'with authority'. He was not like ordinary Jewish teachers, who could debate and then expound the meaning of scripture but would not dare to say anything on their own authority. Jesus spoke as a man in direct touch with God.

Despite this, the way Jesus does refer to the scriptures is very striking. One has only to begin reading the New Testament at the beginning to see how involved with the scriptures he is. It is words from a Psalm and from Isaiah which address him at his baptism (Matthew 3.17). It is commands from Deuteronomy which he quotes to the Devil during his temptation (4.1–11). It is a prophecy in Isaiah which guides the direction of his ministry (4.12–17). His description of true happiness reflects the Psalms and Isaiah (5.3–8). He sums up his aim as to make the teachings of the law and prophets come true; the smallest detail of the law will not be done away with (5.17–18). Now it is Matthew who makes this point most explicit (and he goes on to accompany it with a description of the more radical demands of Jesus's own teaching, 5.21–48). But his picture of Jesus's reliance on the Old Testament with regard to his theology, his living, his ministry, and his teaching is not essentially different from the one which pervades all the gospels.

This being the case, it naturally follows that we can only understand Jesus and the New Testament writers if we understand the assumptions they make on the basis of the Old Testament. Jesus's mission, for instance, is spoken of in terms of the Messiah and the Son of Man, and the ultimate background of these titles lies in the Old Testament's hope of a kingly redeemer, a new David, or of a new man, such as the human figure in Daniel's vision (Daniel 7). The way the New Testament speaks of these figures also reflects Jewish thinking of later times; but it is their presence in the Old Testament that makes these figures inevitable to the New Testament's understanding of Jesus. The scriptures provide the framework for understanding him. So we need the Old Testament to tell us how the New Testament saw the question to which Jesus was the answer. The Old Testament describes the problem and the way it needed to be solved: Jesus comes and declares himself to be the one to solve it.

2. THE OLD TESTAMENT IS THE STORY OF A FAILURE

In describing the Old Testament as setting up the questions to which Jesus is the answer, we acknowledge that the Old Testament has no final answer to the questions it sets. It is incomplete.

The New Testament has several ways of making this point. We may consider them by reviewing some of the sections of this book. First, as a story, the main account of the events from creation through the exodus and occupation of Palestine to the exile is a story with a dead end. God made the world, he tried to redeem the world, but he apparently failed.

The law of the priests underlines the failure in two ways. In its religious aspects, it provides various rituals for dealing with sin. But how can rituals really deal with the obstacles to fellowship between God and man? 'The blood of bulls and goats can never take away sins' (Hebrews 10.4). The rituals only really draw attention to the problem! The law does this in a more general sense. It was given to Israel to obey, and obeying it is the key to being blessed by God. But the law itself recognizes that it will not be obeyed (see Deuteronomy 29–32). In later times, the Jews did their best to take the law seriously, and fell into the opposite trap. They tried to make their obedience the basis of their relationship with God – to earn his approval. Jesus and Paul both speak harsh words about this false devotion to the law. Once again the giving of the law is a failure. It cannot be obeyed, or it leads to wrong attitudes to God.

The advice of the wise men also leads to a dead end. Proverbs and the Song of Songs give impressive descriptions of what life is intended to be like, or should be like, or could be like; but Job and Ecclesiastes protest that the descriptions do not ring true. This is not what it *is* like. Here the questions about the meaning of human life are faced more radically than anywhere else in the Bible, but Job and Ecclesiastes are better at questions than answers, and can only offer trust in the mystery of God.

The words of the prophets and the visions of the seers can look beyond present failure to the glorious consummation of God's purpose. But the glorious consummation keeps being put off. Jeremiah, for instance, promises that the covenant, broken by the exile, will be renewed; the law will now be written on men's hearts, so that they really will obey it. Yet this does not happen. But nowhere is the paradoxical incompleteness of the Old Testament more noticeable than in the promises of Isaiah 40–55. Here is a wonderful vision of the desert turned into pools of water and a profound grasp of the cost that will be involved in the redeeming of man, in the picture of the suffering servant. But the desert is not turned into pools of water, and there is no one to be the suffering servant.

If the Old Testament is the story of a plan of salvation that never came true, of what value is it? The Christian can appreciate it from two perspectives. One is that it describes to him the predicament from which he did need redemption. Every exposure of the depth of sin can make us more appreciative of what God achieved in Christ. The Old Testament shows how deep man's need was.

The other perspective is that Christians have to see themselves as potentially in the same position as Old Testament Israel. They cannot assume that Old Testament Israel was cast off for ever, while the church has now taken her place. On the contrary, God still plans to save Israel, and if the church does not remain faithful, she can be cast off as Israel was (see Romans 11.22–27). So Israel's story is full of warnings for the church.

3. THE OLD TESTAMENT IS OUR STORY

The incompleteness of the Old Testament can be seen as a negative – it constitutes its failure. But it can also be seen as a positive. The whole Bible story is one which moves from creation through the outworking of human sin to the achievement of salvation. It is like a play with several acts. The final act is the coming of Jesus. The earlier acts are the events described in the Old Testament. But they are all scenes from the same play. In describing the Bible story as a play, of course, we do not imply it did not happen. Rather, it is just that, like a play, it has a beginning a middle and an end. All the scenes belong to the same play. And a Christian sees the earlier scenes as just as much part of his story as the last scene is. Although Jesus himself does not appear till the end of the story, even the earlier events were scripted by the God and Father of our Lord Jesus Christ who is also Yahweh, the God of Israel.

As the New Testament sometimes draws attention to the discontinuity between Old and New Testaments (the Old Testament as a dead end), so it sometimes draws attention to the continuity and development from the one to the other. It assumes that over the whole Bible one overarching purpose was operative. It assumes that the Old Testament looks forward to the New and hints at what becomes explicit there. Often, as in a play, the significance of earlier scenes or remarks can only be fully understood in the light of the denouement in the last act.

The Old Testament sacrificial system, for instance, described in Leviticus, is seen in Hebrews as not merely constituting the means by which God's people expressed their relationship to him. It is also (the Christian can see) a hint of the way Jesus's self-sacrifice was to heal the relationship between man and God. The kings (especially David) are not merely leaders in Israel in their day who enjoy a specially close relationship with God and are the means of God blessing Israel and (so it was intended) exercising his lordship over the world. They also hint at how Jesus Christ (the word Christ or messiah means 'anointed' and is a description of kings such as David) will manifest the closest possible relationship with God and be the means of God's blessing the world and exercising his lordship over it. Of course these hints were not necessarily apparent at the time; but one can see them as one looks back from the end of the play.

Sometimes the Old Testament does explicitly look forward. There are many passages in the prophets which see that Israel's present experience, and in particular the way the kings function, does not match up to what God had promised; and these passages look forward to a time when Israel will be put right materially and spiritually, when a real David will sit on the throne. Although the prophecies do look forward, nevertheless they generally see things in terms of a fulfilment or restoration of what the people have lost or never quite experienced. The prophets do not have a chronological telescope which takes them to Galilee and Jerusalem in Jesus's day. But they hint at the great climax to which the story is to come.

In the light of this aspect of the relationship between the Old Testament and the New, the Christian reads the Old Testament as the earlier part of his story. It points forward to Jesus. And it also speaks to the Christian as he, too, lives in the midst of a story which is not yet completed. Although the most important event, the coming of Christ, is passed, we still look forward (as the Old Testament did) to the complete fulfilment of God's purpose for the world.

4. THE OLD TESTAMENT ILLUSTRATES GOD AT WORK

So far we have emphasized the differences between the Testaments. The New Testament also assumes, however, that in the Old the same God is at work, relating to the same people as are spoken of in the New. The Church is not a new entity; it is the rebirth of Israel. So the way God related to Israel in Old Testament times will illustrate how he may be expected to relate to reborn Israel.

We have noted, for instance, in suggesting that the sacrificial system contains hints of what Christ was to achieve, that the sacrifices were also significant in their own right in expressing the relationship between God and his people. The sacrifices burnt whole suggest the giving over to God of ourselves and what is precious to us. The fellowship-offerings illustrate the relationship of gratitude for prayers answered or just for God's love and provision. The sin-offerings remind us of the seriousness of what comes between us and God.

Part of the usefulness of the Old Testament here is that it covers a much wider range of situations than the New. The external circumstances and the attitudes of God's people vary considerably over the range of the Old Testament, and sometimes we have more chance of finding ourselves in the Old Testament than in the narrower confines of the New. For instance, the varied descriptions of the rebellions of God's people, especially in Numbers, suggest features which may still characterize the life of the church. Books such as Job and Ecclesiastes illustrate believers wrestling with doubt. The Psalms embody the praise and prayer of the people of God, and give us hymns and prayers we can actually use, as well as providing models for the prayer and praise that we compose. Paul declares that 'everything written in the Scriptures' (the Old Testament) 'was written to teach us, in order that we might have hope through the patience and encouragement which the Scriptures give us' (Romans 15.4).

5. THE OLD TESTAMENT HAS A BROADER RANGE OF CONCERNS THAN THE NEW

The point just made can be extended in another direction. The number of subjects on which the Old Testament has something to say is larger than is the case with the New. The point is illustrated by simply noting where the Old Testament begins, with creation. It thus explicitly concerns itself with a story set on the widest canvas. Now the New Testament refers to creation, but it does not overtly develop an understanding of the creation relationship between God and the world. It does not need to, because it can presuppose the one which is there in the Old Testament. The strength of the New Testament is that it concentrates all its attention on Jesus. But this is a limitation in so far as it does not tell us so much about God's relationship to the world as a whole.

Because it emphasizes God's creative work, the Old Testament has a very positive attitude to the world itself. Although it sees the world as in a sense spoilt through man's sin, it still sees it as God's world. It believes that God is the Lord of world history, and thus it discusses how he is involved in the affairs of the nations – not just in so far as they relate to Israel, but for the sake of the nations themselves and of God's own concern for righteousness.

God's involvement with and concern for this world appears also in the Old Testament's burden for righteousness in society, which is emphasized by the prophets. The Old Testament does not assume, as Greek thinking tended to do, that God is interested only in the soul – the body being merely the dispensable packaging for the really important inner man. It believes body and spirit were both given by God, both to be paid attention to, and both in the end to be saved. Thus it is concerned with the spirit, with man's relationship with God. But it is also concerned with his bodily welfare and his bodily behaviour.

As Christians have read the Old Testament, they have sometimes concluded that its concern with the outward man marks it as inferior and unspiritual. But if God really is the creator, we can learn from the Old Testament how to have a right concern for and enjoyment of the world.

6. THE OLD TESTAMENT SHOWS GOD CONDESCENDING TO MAN'S WEAKNESS

We have noted that, although Jesus in Matthew (5.17) declares that no part of the Law is to be done away with, he also declares that whereas people were told one thing in the past, he is now telling them something different. Whereas some of the things he refers to which people were told in the past do not come from the Old Testament (for instance, the addition of 'hate your enemies' to 'love your friends', Matthew 5.43), most of the commands he discusses here do come from the scriptures. The law includes provision for divorce; Jesus speaks of divorce as leading to legalized adultery (5.31–32). The law speaks of 'an eye for an eye and a tooth for a tooth'; Jesus urges offering the left cheek to the person who slaps the right cheek (5.38–39).

In both these passages Jesus is asserting a more radical demand than the one the law made. The law took a realistic view of the fact that divorces happen, and sought to provide regulations to protect the wife. Jesus does not abrogate the law in the sense of saying that there is no need to bother with the wife's protection. He goes deeper into the question and declares that divorce should not happen. Similarly, the law took a realistic view of the fact that men seek vengeance for wrongs done to them, and sought to limit that vengeance (one black eye, not two, in return for one inflicted!). Jesus does not abrogate the law in the sense of freeing people like Lamech (Genesis 4.23–24) to be as vengeful as they like. He goes deeper into the question and declares that vengeance is not to be indulged in at all; indeed self-giving is the rule.

What is illustrated here is that the Old Testament starts where men are; we have noted this point in chapter 9. The laws are given to cope with the kind of eventualities that will arise in human society. Then Jesus comes and says that human society ought to have an entirely different basis. He can say this because his own aim is to give it a new basis. His dying to bring men God's forgiveness and his rising to give them God's Holy Spirit opens up new possibilities for the realization of God's ideal, and this is what he calls men to.

But where is God's ideal revealed? In Christ, of course; but also in the Old Testament. This point is most clearly made in his later discussion of marriage and divorce (Matthew 19.1–12). His declaration that in an ideal world divorces will not happen at all is based not on his own ideas but on the account of the origin of the marriage relationship in Genesis. The Old Testament contains both God's ideal, and his condescension to man's weakness.

We need both of these. We need God's ideal to summon us to the ultimate standard we are called to aim at in Christ. We need God's realistic lower standard for some insight on how to modify God's ideals to the world in which we actually have to live. And we also need them for ourselves, for although God's forgiveness and God's Holy Spirit are given to us, we do carry on living in this age with the pressures of the old nature, and even we might find God's ideals self-defeating if they were all we had. But God meets us in our weakness too, and the Old Testament illustrates this.

What is true of the Old Testament is true of the Bible as a whole. It is God's story: it invites us to treat this as our story. It is God's word: it invites us to hear this word as addressed to us. It is the response of God's people: it invites us to make that response our own.